THE BLUE ROAD

THE BLUE ROAD

KENNETH WHITE

MAINSTREAM
PUBLISHING

First published in France as *La Route Bleue*
Published in Great Britain 1990 by
MAINSTREAM PUBLISHING COMPANY (EDINBURGH) LTD
7 Albany Street
Edinburgh EH1 3UG
ISBN 1 85158 279 7 (cloth)

British Library Cataloguing in Publication Data

White, Kenneth
The blue road.
I. Title II. La route bleue. *English*

823'.914 [F]

ISBN 1-85158-279-7

Typeset in 10/11 Garamond by
Novatext Graphix Limited, Edinburgh
Printed in Great Britain by
Martins of Berwick, Berwick-Upon-Tweed

For the Great Work Field

The greatest characteristic of the present age is that it is stale — stale as literature. To enter a new world, and have there freedom of movement and newness.

William Carlos Williams

Travelling I consider as an extremely useful exercise. It sets the mind in movement.

Montaigne

Me, I'm a Redskin, with a blue belly and a head of gold. I'm lighting out, I'm heading for the hills — the hills of the soul.

Joseph Delteil

All kinds of tunes, even on metaphysical trips.

Rimbaud

Real culture can only be learned in space. Space culture means the culture of a mind that breathes and has its being in space, and that calls into itself all the bodies that move in space, making them the very objects of its thought.

Antonin Artaud

Blue soul, dark road.

Georg Trakl

He's always got to go a bit farther on; that's his only home.

Georges Bataille

The stranger's out on the road, ahead of everybody else. He isn't just wandering about, with nowhere to go. All the time, he's coming closer to the place he can call his own.

Martin Heidegger

We've been out on the way. Now the snow is falling, in a million flakes. Several scrolls of blue mountain have just been painted.

Shôbôgenzô

CONTENTS

PREFACE

I got the call from Labrador, the land that God gave Cain, as Captain Cartier called it, when I was eleven years old. It was all because of a book and the images it contained: of Indians, Eskimos, mountains, fish and white wolves howling at the moon.

So, you get images fixed in your mind when you're eleven years old (you can think yourself lucky it was that kind of image you got), and you follow them up thirty years later, having accomplished in the meantime several more or less erratic, more or less fertile excursions into the fields of life and knowledge.

That's how I got on to this blue road.

But what's a 'blue road'? I hear somebody asking.

I'm not too sure about that myself. There's the blue of the big sky, of course, there's the blue of the river, the mighty St Lawrence, and, later on, there's the blue of the ice. But all those notions, along with a few others I can think of, while they talk to my senses and my imagination, still don't exhaust the depth of that 'blue'.

So it's something mystic then?

I wouldn't want to get involved in palaver about that word at this juncture (there's something a whole lot fresher calling us out), but if I let my mind dwell for a moment on this kind of vocabulary, I recall that in some of the old traditions they talk of the *itinerant* mystic, and they say that if a man caught up in 'Western exile' wants to find his 'Orient', he has to go through a passage North.

Maybe the blue road is that passage North, among the blues of silent Labrador.

Maybe the idea is to go as far as possible — to the end of yourself — till you get into a territory where time turns into space, where things appear in all their nakedness and the wind blows anonymously.

Maybe.

Anyway, I wanted to get out there, up there, and *see.*

K. W.

THE MOON IN MONTREAL

We've got so much space and so little time, only one thing to do: turn nomad.
Annie Lebrun

'One egg sunny side, toast 'n' coffee!'

That's Montreal out there, and I like the way it sounds: the streets, the river, the voices. And way far back of it all, silent and beautiful, Labrador.

I start asking questions about Labrador straight after breakfast. At the Bus Terminal, I pick up one of the phones you can get information through and, as though I were eleven years old, I say:

'Excuse me, how can I get to Labrador?'

'To *where?*'

'Labrador.'

'*Labrador!*'

'That's right, Labrador.'

'Look, mister, is this a joke or something?'

'Not a bit, I'm serious!'

'OK, so you're crazy.'

'I beg your pardon?'

'Where do you come from, mister?'

'France.'

'That's what I thought. Mister, where you come from, the provinces stick close together. Here, it's different.'

'Okay, So it's different. But just tell me how to get there.'

'Mister, I just don't know. My job is to answer reasonable questions.'

And she hangs up on me.

What's unreasonable about Labrador? I mean, it isn't just a figment of the imagination. It's a place, right? And if it's a place, that means you can go there, no? Or at least get near it, make an approach to it, no? Apparently, *no.*

I felt as if I'd asked a metaphysical question at a congress of logical positivists:

'Does paradise exist?'

'Get that dingo outa here!'

I shove a quarter in a convenient slot and watch TV for a while, craftily working out the next move.

Got to be more subtle about it, more sophisticated. I saunter into a café and get into talk with the waitress. I prepare the ground very carefully. She knows I come from France, she knows I arrived in Montreal yesterday, she knows all about the flight, I tell her about the big blunt-nosed Boeing and all the passengers, I even get back to General de Gaulle and that's almost archaeology, when she says:

'What you aim to do in Quebec?'

I seize my opportunity.

'I want to go to Labrador.'

'It's cold up there.'

'Maybe you're too used to central heating.'

'Maybe you thought we were all Eskimos?'

It's too much to say I'm getting hot. But at least this citizen doesn't just wipe Labrador off the map. She's come out with an epithet, and when you can come out with an epithet, that means you recognize, however vaguely, a substantive. It's elementary grammar, and you've got to be able to stand on something. Even the Hopis do it.

That night around midnight — there's a big round Autumn moon sailing grandly over Montreal — I'm eating onion soup at a little spot on the Rue St Denis in the company of a Quebec writer when I put the question to him point-blank:

'How come Labrador isn't a reality in Montreal?'

He goes into a long socio-ethnological explanation. What it all boils down into is that, for him, the Quebec people are all peasants from Poitou who still haven't come alive to the fact that they've arrived on the American continent. They're culturally traumatised and haven't even begun to get their bearings in the new space. They spend their time remembering. The motto of

Quebec is *Je me souviens* (I remember).

I asked somebody what the remembering was all about:

'The time the English came.'

God almighty! Who cares about the English, whether coming or going?

If I bothered about what the English did, I'd be up there in old Caledonia with a historical chip on my shoulder, scrawling long political poems in Lallans and waving a wee flag.

Shit, you can't be a Scotsman *all* your life. At least, you can't always be harping on it. You've got to get out there and mix it more. *Make* something of it.

The next night, I'm mixing it with a little Canadian girl, part French, part Scot, part Mohawk, up in Outremont.

Mademoiselle Pocahontas MacGregor.

She was really something.

But I've got Labrador on the brain, so before very long, I bring up the subject once more:

'I really want to get up there, into Labrador.'

'Give over,' she says. 'Every time I hear you say that word, I get a chill up my spine.'

And she actually shivers.

But my allusion to Labrador has gone deeper with her than a shiver down the back, it's wakened live images in her mind. For a few minutes later she's telling me about wild duck flying at 300 mph against the wind. . . . And when I pursue with what my writer-friend said about the Quebec people, she thinks for a moment and then she says:

'The Quebec folk are gentle, but strange.'

At the time, that seemed to me an extraordinarily beautiful phrase.

Maybe I should have mentioned the fact that we were royally stoned. And since the idea of that was for me to get inside info about Labrador, I mean direct info from the Collective Unconscious and the Oversoul, and maybe the Archaean rocks that must be continually sending out vibrations, mostly into thin air, because nobody's smart enough to pick 'em up, I had a notebook and a pencil handy, and every time that little Canadienne said something, I was so scared I'd forget it, I'd heave over and note it in the dark (not too easy, but I'd chosen a notebook with big pages — sometimes I think of everything).

'What you doing there on the other side of the bed?'

'I'm noting down the moment's reality.'

'Reality? What's that?'

This time it was my turn to have a delicious little metaphysical shiver running up my spine.

I was beginning to feel myself in my element. I was beginning to love Canada. I mean Quebec. That's one of the queer things up here: you can't say Canada. If you as much as whisper that word, you're a British imperialist pig. You got to say Quebec. So let me get it straight once and for all. If I happen to say 'Canada' when I should be saying 'Quebec', it's not politics, I just like the sound of the word better, OK?

I was beginning to love Quebec. I loved it all night. That big round moon was driving me crazy.

In the morning the little Quebec girl ups with a rush and says:

'I got to split. See you tonight.'

I take a stroll through the chill-red atmosphere of early morning Outremont, then go downtown.

Montreal isn't a high town. There are more than a few high-risers, but it's still a human-sized place. I find myself walking along leaf-scuffling streets, past rows of bright-coloured two-storey houses, feeling all around me the raw spaciousness that is America.

I go into a bar.

'A beer.'

'What brand?'

'The best.'

'Everything's relative, but okay . . .'

He gives me a Molson Brador.

Now, if you've been following me, phonetically as well as philosophically (and if you haven't, you'll never be a new world traveller, not in a hundred years), if, then, you've been following me phonetically: bar, Brador, Labrador . . . you will know that we are now approaching the heart of the matter.

This guy had actually *been* to Labrador.

He was one of us.

He had a brother worked in the iron ore mines at Labrador City, and he'd been up there on a fishing trip. He said you could go pretty far up by bus, and then there was the train from Seven Islands that went climbing right up to Schefferville. And from Seven Islands too you could get a little plane to Fort Chimo, Goose Bay or Davis Inlet. It was clear, high music in my ears.

Talking about music, the piece that was playing then and there on the juke box was Duke Ellington telling the world to take the A train. . .

But I was in no hurry. I continued strolling round Montreal.

When Henry Thoreau was in Montreal (he didn't spend *all* his time on the banks of Walden Pond), his Protestant snitch smelled Catholic incense everywhere. It still lingers: the church of *Marie-Reine-du-Monde*, the *Centre d'Animation Missionnaire* . . . but there's less of it, a whole lot less. Quebec got de-Catholicised overnight a few years ago, according to my writer friend. They call it the Quiet Revolution. The Quiet Quebecois just woke up one fine morning and realized he was liberated. Jesus! No more original sin. The great god Pan making a comeback. Joints in place of holy wafers, poems in place of confessions. And fuck the pope even if he's Polish. They talk of Cuba, but Cuba's old hat compared to Quebec. Quebec had something better than a revolution. Up here, they almost made it the whole way from agitation to apocalypse, from culture drama to the cosmic dream.

Almost . . .

But they could really invent something extraordinary up here, if they could only stop once and for all being Poitou peasants. America's other chance. France's other chance. Who knows, maybe the planet's other chance.

I talked along those lines with the owner of a bookshop called Quebec-America. There was somebody who had the right idea! Not Quebec-France, nor Quebec-United States, nor Quebec-Quebec, but Quebec-America. We got on to Melville. Melville seemed to him as to me the very type of the extravagant Euro-American: the man who jumps over two or three mental frontiers and finds himself in the middle of a great nowhere, at which moment he looks around in wonder and comes out with something really illuminating and mind-opening like: *Thar she blows!*

That's right, the white whale and the big winds: Labrador.

I've been making for Labrador since I could walk. Took to the Labrador road straight from the cradle.

'There is,' notes Thoreau in *A Natural History of Massachusetts*, 'a singular health in these words, Labrador and East Maine, which no desponding creed recognizes.'

Right.

And he comes back on Labrador in *A Winter Walk*:

'Let a brave, devout man spend the year in the woods of Maine or Labrador, and see if the Hebrew Scriptures speak adequately to his condition and experience, from the setting in of Winter to the breaking up of the ice.'

You see what I'm after and what I'm up to.

For years I've been trying to get out from under a big book and all the mind-fuzz it engendered. I've been trying to make my way out of the Jehovian occupation of the world. All clear now. But there remains the final step. That's Labrador.

Labrador is where I come full circle, swallow my birth, develop all the negatives of my adolescence and get a good look at my original face. What I need above all at the moment is space, a big white breathing space for the ultimate meditation.

SPACE.

I've been to Maine, by the way. That just whetted my appetite for Labrador.

QUEBEC CITY FLASH

I was all tense and excited, like I was going to rob a bank. Till I just dropped the score and began to improvise. Then, by God, it was all as smooth as a dream.

Mezz Mezzrow, *Really the Blues*

The driver of the taxi that took me to the bus terminal was Indian. It was at the red traffic light we got into conversation. His eye was on the light, his foot was on the pedal, and he was rarin' to go:

'Need a good car,' he muttered, half to himself.

'This a good car?'

'You bet. Chevrolet. Light. They *go*. I put the super-gas. I want *power*. You got to . . .'

The traffic light changed and he was off.

'. . . have pick-up.'

Then he added, after some reflection:

'This is a crazy job, you know. It is a sickness.'

On a wall surrounding a wasteland somebody has painted in big scarlet letters:

CHRIST
WILL RETURN
IN
1986
THE ST LAWRENCE
WILL RUN WITH BLOOD

Yet another psychotic Christian. World's full of 'em. They pollute the air. You nutcase, go away and read Teilhard de Chardin. After that, read Walt Whitman. And rendezvous in Labrador.

The great outside.

At the terminal, I check out the buses for Quebec City. I notice there are two routes, and I choose the longer one. When I go to buy my ticket, the man says:

'Going to Quebec? You know there's an express?'

I say, sure, I know there's an express. But I don't like to make haste with my travelling, I try to make the most of it. Then, as if there was some kind of logic in the remark (and maybe there is), I add:

'I'm going to Labrador.'

'There's nothin' up there.'

End of conversation.

I watch a Greyhound Americruiser slide out for New York, then board my *Voyageur* for Quebec.

Americruising and voyageuring . . .

It's one of those cloud-dappled days that make you think of Gerard Manley Hopkins.

We glide by:

Canadian Pacific
Molson's Brewery
Imperial Molasses
Grandma Food Products
Sucre St Laurent
Georgia Pacific
Canada West India Molasses Co.
Alliance Steel Corporation . . .

Out on the choppy, green, and sparkling river, the big cargos are waiting:

Gaspé Transport

Athol Monarch
Overseas Aleutian

The sense of a world wide open. The sense of raw materials. The sense of American space.

The senses. Can't get deep enough into them. But before you even try to get into them, the thing to do is open 'em, all of 'em. Maybe one big overall sense in the end. But don't be too anxious to make unities either. Keep it all plural and moving. An open coherence . . . We don't want God or the One muscling in on us again. Even if we get back to the One, it won't be the same one.

These little bits of nascent thought — like the patches of sunlight darting over the St Lawrence — are going through my head as we pass through:

Bout de l'île
Maskinongé Junction
Louiseville
Yamachiche
Pointe du Lac
Baie Jolie. . . .

Me too, I'm in love with American names!

At Trois-Rivières, there's a fifteen-minute stop. I drink a philosophical coffee in the company of Ludwig Wittgenstein ('What you can't talk about, *shows itself,*') then go for a stroll in the street. At the windy corner of Des Forges and Du Fleuve, I watch the St Lawrence rolling by. Another big cargo out there:

Logistic Transport.

Ah, how the world always seems to be throwing out signs. Logistic transports!

We continue on our way:

Cap-de-la-Madeleine
Tabagie Jules
Champlain
Batiscan
Donnaconna . . .

The woods we've been going through are riotous with colour: red, yellow, orange, redorange, darkyellowred. Sheer delight for the eyes out there in the sun and the wind. Maples, yes, but also birch, larch, fir. How come the birches seem so much whiter here? As if even the scientific name *Betula alba* ought to take a little fling to itself and turn into an ecstatic *Betula albissima albissima.* Must be the influence of Labrador, shedding its whiteness over the world.

'Take the A train.' Maybe you wondered what the A stands for? I'll tell you:

America
Atopia
Anarchic
Anachronistic
Anomic . . .

The A-way means neither history, poetry nor philosophy. None of those old words. Something else.

Absolutely.

All along the road, you've seen those stolid fellows with the skip caps and the rocking chairs, rocking on their self-made-man verandahs. You've seen those piled-up stalls of red Mackintosh apples and the ruddy-faced Canadiennes standing sturdily beside them. Mackintosh apples, maple syrup, furs. It's Autumn in America. Autumn, 'season of mellow fruitfulness' (remember?). But those furs came out of Labrador. Johnny the poet never got as far as that. For *that* space, you need another language, and to find that language you've got to follow right to the end the trail of the red leaves.

L'Ancienne Lorette Junction
Sainte-Foy
Quebec City

I feel like hanging around the bus-station for a while, so I go into the little restaurant and eat a coffee-and-pie, listening to the neo-French voice of Quebec:

'*C'est une gang de bums . . .*'

'*Mon char est scrappé . . .*'

'*Une beurrée de beurre de peanut . . .*'

I follow up the coffee-and-pie with a *pouding au riz à la maple syrup*, still keeping my ears open:

'*J'ai blowé . . .*'

'*Tabarnac !*'

'*Je vais gazer . . .*'

then take a taxi in the flaming sunset for Cap Rouge, bombing along the Boulevard Duplessis and the Chemin de Ste-Foy. It's at Cap Rouge that another writer lives who's going to be giving me his hospitality for the next few days.

There's a slender birch-tree growing just outside my window. Reminds me of Pocahontas MacGregor. When I waken in the morning, it's to see the sunlight flashing on its bark.

Semaphore from the unknown.

Logistic transports again.

At Quebec, I want to do three things. Visit the Château de Frontenac? Nah. Do a remembrance visit to the Heights of Abraham? Nope. You're all wet. I'm going to get me a good map of Labrador, pay a visit to the *Centre d'Etudes Nordiques* (Centre for Northern Studies) at Laval, and take a look at the Huron reservation over Ancienne Lorette way. I am beginning to get organised.

As you've guessed already, getting hold of a map of Labrador was no easy matter. I could get maps with all the one-horse towns between Montreal and New York. I could get maps of the US, Ottawa-supervised Canada, Province of Quebec, faraway France, Germany, Britain, Japan. But Labrador, nothing doing. The place was beginning to look even more far-out and impossible than I'd thought. Not even a map . . .

I *almost* got hold of a map of Labrador at the *Ministère des Terres et Forêts* (the Forestry Commission), but the said *Ministère* was just closing down for the weekend and would I please come back Monday? I'm on the threshold of paradise, and they say will you please come back Monday!

Institutions and individuals will never be on the same wavelength.

That's why I'm an anarchist.

A *laughing* anarchist.

The man I talk with at the *Centre d'Etudes Nordiques* has just come down from Indian House Lake. Archaeologist. When I ask him about books on Labrador, he starts off by telling me there's next to nothing. But after I've quizzed him for about an hour, followed by a couple of hours conscientious research in the library, I have a bibliography of about fifty titles. Enough to be going on with. And a map of Labrador.

'What you going to do with all that?'

'Write a poem.'

'I didn't know poets worked like that.'

'I don't come from Poitou.'

Don't get me wrong. I've got nothing against Poitou. It's Pictland, after all — if you go back far enough. Which means these people are my cousins. But regionalist ideology never goes back far enough. It never goes back further than Granma.

A little later, still thinking on those things, I'm sitting in the restaurant *Le Gaulois* when my eye, as it scans the menu, comes across *la soupe du barde*. The soup of the bard! I order it, with me right thumb on me left wisdom tooth (according to ye olde Celtic custom). Because in France, if you come from Scotland, Ireland, Wales or Brittany, or anywhere else on the Celtic fringe, and scribble a page or two, you're a bard. Sooner or later some critic looking for a gimmick is going to call you a bard. No wonder Yeats called journalism the ruin of literature. Let's get it straight, boys, once and for all. A bard is one who sings and re-sings the history of the tribe. Being without a tribe, and doing my damnedest to get *out* of history, I just can't be no beardy bard, OK?

Call me Ishmael, intellectual nomad.

I don't know whether I'm *looking* for a tribe. I don't think so (I prefer the company of secret and solitary minds like Scot Erigena and Duns Scot), but it's true I'm kind of interested in tribes right now. Maybe because I've had a bellyful of nations and states.

Which brings us, naturally, to the Huron village.

'You pass an Irving, and you continue straight on. Then you see a curve, then you cross a bridge.'

Such were the directions given to my writer-friend who was doing the driving that afternoon. And sure enough, there's the petrol station, here's the curve and there's the bridge.

Now, as every schoolboy knows, the word Huron was made in France. It comes from *hure*, meaning 'boar's head', and refers to the way those wild Iroquois wore their hair. As to the word Iroquois, it's at least in part original Indian. It comes from the word *iro*, meaning 'I have spoken', which is what the Indians always said after they'd made a little speech. And they were always making little speeches, those Indians. The Indian became taciturn only after he'd been practically beaten into the ground.

Gros-Louis, the reservation chief, isn't taciturn.

He's not only voluble, he's articulate.

He's even written a book, and here's what he says in it:

'I am indignant at the legislation that gave the province of Quebec an official flag that has nothing to do with the province. Why choose as our emblem those white lilies that have never grown here and never will? No, that flag will never fly over our reservation! I swore an oath to myself to do everything in my power to prevent it. The best way to thwart their plans was to put together a flag that represented us, one that would truly symbolise our activities and our way of life. I could see in my mind's eye the flag I would impose when circumstances permitted: the skin of a black bear with a snowshoe in the middle. To show that we were the ones who had created it, I would put an Indian head right in the centre of the snowshoe. Then to emphasize it, there would be an Indian canoe floating across the blue water that reflected our sky, as blue in Winter as in Summer. My dream has been realised and this flag flies over our Huron reservation, protecting our being and our people with all its traditions and its pride.'

I don't care much for flags, one way or the other, but when I hear Gros-Louis declare that he wants to waken his people from three centuries of lethargy, I find myself thinking: three centuries, that's not so long — how long have we been sleeping in Europe?

In Gros-Louis' Indian museum you can contemplate a mocassin that they say belonged to Sitting Bull himself. But you don't have to believe them. They're all a bunch of tricksters and they like making jokes.

They have a pre-Columbian sense of comedy.

Redskinned Rabelais!

ROUTE 175 NORTH

A number of ancients died on the road. I myself have long been tempted by the cloud-moving wind.

Matsuo Bashô

Out from Quebec City.

Route 175 North.

I like the bare mathematics of it, between the two charged words.

The calculable and the incalculable.

A colder spell had set in. It had been a summery Autumn, but now suddenly there was a sharp Winter's bite in the air.

November chill blaws lood wi' angry sugh . . .

Funny how a line of Robert Burns should come into my head. Maybe the ghost of some Scotsman who trekked up here before me? I was to come across Scotch traces all over the place, and I met up with more than one Indian with a name like Jean-Baptiste Mackenzie.

Rolling through the Laurentides.

To the west there, the river Jacques-Cartier, which will later give way to the river Chicoutimi. All around, the woods: reddy, orangy, with white flashes from the birch.

I was pretty sure I'd already said all I'd ever want to say about birches. The number of pages I've written on birches! I thought I knew them inside out, all the way, from botany to mythology. But last night I read something in the story of an Indian trapper that gave my mind a jolt. In winter, the white bark of the birches *takes on a rosy tint*.

In some patches, the frost is lying thick.
Into the frost world . . .
Haiku country.

The Autumn Wind
blows along the stones
on Mount Asama

Altitude 2305 metres.

The waters of Lac Jacques-Cartier are grey and agitated, and the wind is sweeping great black fans across it.

Like Whistler's portrait of Carlyle.

Kelvingrove Art Gallery, Glasgow.

Leaving the university, coming down the hill, to breathe a clearer atmosphere, get in touch with something farther out. Grey afternoon. Cold silence of the galleries. The portrait of Carlyle, all grey and black.

Talking to that big man.

Who was reading Carlyle's highflying extravaganzas in a land gone flat? Me. Born of a planet that was freezing above Kelvin Park. Me, the emigrant of Great Western Road.

Altitude 874 metres.

Lac Grelon
Lac Beloeil
Lac Davis
Lac Tourangeau
Lac des Uries . . .

The Lake Poets.

Wordsworth.

'A plainer and more emphatic language . . . the beautiful and permanent forms of nature . . .'

But 'too tame for the Chippewa', says Thoreau.

Wild iris
so many Springs ago
not even the shadow of mankind

Those who follow the North road, trying to get into the clear, beyond all the fuzz.

On the 20th January, 1778, the poet Lenz took the road leading up into the mountains . . .

Nietzsche followed him.

And Rimbaud.

And Artaud . . .

Lenz collapsed on a street in Moscow. Nietzsche broke down in Turin. Rimbaud lay cursing blue murder in a Marseilles hospital. Artaud wound up in a howling academy at Ivry.

The far-out men of Europe. Erratic suns, looking for their cosmos . . .

Signposts announce the presence of caribou.

Here's what a certain John Maclean wrote around 1840 about the caribou migrations:

'They make their appearance in March, coming from the West, and direct their course over the barren grounds near the coast until they reach George's River, where they halt. In the month of October, the does follow the banks of George's River until they meet the bucks. The whole then proceed together, through the interior, to the place whence they came.'

Men watch them and imagine the Great Home of the Caribou, and Caribou Man, lord of the animals, who dwells in the far North . . .

Myths to live by.

Myths, the sacred — blasted.

So, the flattened-out landscape of the last men, rife with rootless knowledge, hysteria and boredom?

Or *something else.*

'A pure animal man would be lovely as a deer, burning like a flame fed straight from underneath. And he'd be part of the unseen. He'd breathe silence and he'd never cease to wonder.'

Brother Lawrence.

Just before you get to Chicoutimi, you find the River Ha! Ha! and Lake Ha! Ha! Some Indian must have laughed his head off there.

Laughing at what?

Being and nothingness.

The first supernihilist.

Traded with the citizens of Chicoutimi, but had his head in another world.

CHICOUTIMI, COUSCOUS AND OLD WHITE WHISKY

The Orient *sought for by the mystic, an* Orient *marked on none of our maps, lies to the North, beyond the North.*

Henry Corbin

The name of Chicoutimi comes from a Cree word: *chekotimwo*, meaning 'deep water'. Situated on the banks of the river Saguenay, it was an important fur-trading post in the early nineteenth century, the main trading post in all the Montagnais country.

We first hear of it in 1661, in the *Relation* of two Jesuit priests, Gabriel Druillet and Claude Dablon, who accompanied the French expedition sent out in that year to discover a way to Hudson's Bay along the Saguenay and the Lac Saint-Jean:

'We left Tadoussac on 1st June, 1661, with forty canoes, and on the sixth day, early, we arrived at Chicoutimi, a fine-looking place. Here the river-trip ended, and the portages began.'

The bus station is lodged in an abandoned cinema that still bears the grandiloquent name of The Imperial Palace. I get my rucksack from the boot of the car. Since the last trip, it's been enhanced with a grouse claw picked up in Glasgow. Was that for luck or for aesthetics?

I go into a bar down by the harbour and order a whisky.

What a sinister place this is, smelling rankly of stale tobacco and immemorial boredom, with a huge pool table right plunk in the middle of things.

What does boredom look like?

A huge pool table and nobody playing.

Slightly fortified by the whisky, I get out and walk the high noon streets of Chicoutimi.

Dixie Lee's Lunch Counter offers hot dogs and fresh cod. Another spot, the Café Oasis, proposes couscous and merguez.

Sooner or later I'll be looking for a place to eat, but in the meantime I just keep hoofing around, waiting for something to turn up, some little sign to tickle my brain into action . . .

Have a dish of noodles on the spot
and take another one back home

Chinee restaurant, that one.

Realising I'm noticing only restaurants, I decide to go and eat and get that over with so as to be able to think of something else. Make up my mind, for example, whether I'm going to stay the night in Chicoutimi or push on.

I make for the Café Oasis and chew merguez to the tune of a little love-song from the radio that goes like this: '*J'aime tes seins, j'aime tes reins, nous nous aimons comme des chiens.*' About as erotic as a tapeworm.

Just at that moment, a leetle Pocahontas passes by.

Ah, my beauty of the backwoods!

My little mountain rose!

My two-legged American dream!

Gone.

I decide I'm going to stick around anyway.

Haven't given Chicoutimi its chance yet.

After the Oasis, I go visit the local museum. It's a sad fact about so many places nowadays — if you want to get at something live, you've got to go to the museum.

Amazing! It looks as if all the Indians were dressed in tartan. All those Scotch fur-traders must have been flogging them plaids in return for skins. As everybody knows, after the '45 rebellion, the wearing of tartan was prohibited in North Britain, and I used to wonder what they did with all the bloody cloth. Now I know.

I linger before a Montagnais drum, a birch bark canoe, and a rifle with a beaded and embroidered shoulder strap . . .

Neil McLaren (born 1766 at Lochearn, Perthshire) was agent of the North-West Company at Chicoutimi from 1800 to 1805. He kept a journal in which, from day to day, he noted his transactions. He also noted, with typical Scotch thoroughness, the temperature, as well as the force and direction of the wind:

'Tuesday, 12th October 1802. A cold, dark day. East wind, and a thin snow falling. We made up twenty packets for the Lac St-Jean and Asouapmouchouan.'

A 'packet', intended for the trappers in the back country, could contain anything from bullets to whisky, including flour, peas, Indian corn, salt pork, fat, tea, tobacco and clay pipes . . .

McLaren notes how one day he measured out seven barrels of 'Beauport Whisky' into seventy-four pots, adding that this beverage was 'watered down fifty per cent for common usage'. He was not a big drinker himself, McLaren, but he no doubt liked a wee snifter now and then, in which case you may be sure he did not partake of the watered down version 'for common usage'. Not that I imagine him imbibing the same firewater at one hundred per cent. No, I see him rather pouring himself delicately a little refreshment from the keg of another whisky he mentions elsewhere: 'Marc Beaumont's fine *whisky blanc*'.

The furs would start coming in around May-June, when the lakes and rivers were thawed out and the trappers could canoe their skins down to the post.

All kinds of skins, with the gleam of the North still on them: beaver, sable, musk rat, lynx, otter, mink . . .

Imagine them coming down the Saguenay, canoe after canoe. Trapper jumps ashore, undoes his load, makes his bargain, leaves his gun for repair at the forge, blows his money and paddles back to the woods again.

The Indian gradually gets pushed to the side. The intruder has become the inhabitant, and the inhabitant becomes the outcast.

Now and then, one of those lost Indians would turn up at the post, half-starved, crazy:

'Saturday, 23rd January 1802. The Indian Kamashenagush came by today to get flour for a family of Indians on the Islets de Jérémie.'

When, later on in the century, the sawmills started up, tearing away the forest from right under their eyes, the Indians felt it was time to react. They did so very modestly, making a petition to the governor, Lord Elgin, in Quebec:

'Let us be given a piece of land around the Lac Saint-Jean. And stop the foreign savages from cutting down our woods and hunting on our grounds. If you do not grant us what we ask, then we shall disappear, like snow in the Spring sun. I have spoken.'

In 1848, those Montagnais Indians were given a little monetary compensation, ridiculously little. Then, in 1856, a reservation was set out at Pointe-Bleue. That's where I'll be making for in a day or two.

But in the meantime I'm taking it easy in Chicoutimi.

In the evening, I go for a stroll along the Saguenay: grey waters flecked with silver and gold.

It's very beautiful.

Something Indian in the air.

THE WALK TO POINTE-BLEUE

We made this trip to find our life.
Indian Song

We pull out of Chicoutimi on 170 West, from which we soon switch to 169 North, rolling through the Kenogami forest then skirting the Lac Saint-Jean.

I wonder if we'll ever get rid of all this evangelical toponymy. I can't say what this lake's Indian name was, but I'm willing to bet it was beautiful, and precise too. Something like Blue Water Lake, or Summer Storm Lake or Many Tree Lake. Named by people who *knew* it, who were in touch with its physical reality. But Lac Saint-Jean, I ask you. Was St John ever here? Not at all. He hung around Galilee. And the folk who named the lake 'Saint-Jean', they were never really here either. They had the back of their heads glued to a big black book. So they stuck names on the reality, and then got down to a-workin' and a-multiplyin' according to the Law. That's civilisation, whatever be the book or the code. Nothing to do with beautifully felt reality. Which is why Flaubert could say that 'civilisation is a conspiracy against poetry'.

Night falls and I arrive in Dolbeau.

There's a snell wind blowing up the street. Nothing else. Nothing but the wind. Where *is* everybody?

With this special go-to-the-end-of-the-world bus ticket I've got, there are certain hôtels all along the way I can get special conditions in. So naturally I try to locate the hôtel that's on my list.

L'Auberge de la Diligence.

But I pass by one, two, three hôtels without seeing hair nor hide of the 'Stagecoach Inn'.

At length I actually encounter a citizen in the street. Old raggedy Rip Van Winkle kind of character. I ask him where, please, is the *Auberge de la Diligence*? He reflects for a while, with the exaggerated concentration of the drunkard (Granpaw's been at the Tulamore Dew), he reflects, and he better reflects, he ponders and he cogitates, then he brings forth his answer:

'Never seen the place, boy.'

The Stagecoach Inn must have closed its doors just after Buffalo Bill passed by here on his way to Gay Paree.

I checked in at *Le Repos des Chasseurs.*

The room was crummy: a wet towel, a washhand basin smeared with toothpaste, a set of ominous stains on the carpet and a constellation of cigarette holes on the bed cover. The whole place was redolent with sadness, a stale smoke, all-American sadness. You could imagine the deaths of innumerable salesmen . . .

A night in Dolbeau.

I wander about the deserted streets.

In the window of a sports shop, I see a record that tells you how to attract and hunt the elk.

I read the instructions on the sleeve.

Moo-huh, moo-huh-huh . . .

I stand in front of that sports shop window making elky noises. Till I feel I'm in danger of going completely screwy. So I decide to call it a night and go to bed.

The other day in Chicoutimi I picked up a couple of books, and I read them into the wee small hours of the morning. One is V. A. Huard's *Labrador and Anticosti,* written right there in Chicoutimi in 1897, the other is La Hontan's eighteenth-century *Curious Dialogues with a Savage.*

For Father Huard, full of religious unction and humble self-content, the Montagnais Indians are 'the poor children of the woods'. He recognises the ravages that European civilisation has wreaked on them: only a couple of thousand left, and these on their last legs. Within a few years, says the father, they'll be gone entirely. Sad indeed. But there is a bright ray in the picture. The Indian people have entered their death throes, but, 'thanks to the unstinting and unrelenting work of the good missionaries', their death will be edifying. So everything is for the best and we can continue to thank the Lord.

La Hontan is a livelier character, with a more open mind. Born in South-West France in 1666, he landed in Canada in 1683, published an English translation of his *Curious Dialogues with a Savage* at London in 1702 (at the time, London and Amsterdam were the only healthy places for thinking in), and died probably around 1715, God knows where. For La Hontan, writing right in the middle of what was to be called 'the crisis in the European conscience', the Indians, far from being reduced to the paternalised status of 'poor children of the woods', are 'naked philosophers' whose thought and way of life all well in advance of anything that can be found in Europe. In fact, as the 'curious dialogues' proceed, Christianity and European ideology in general look more and more preposterous. 'I am delighted to be able to converse with you,' says La Hontan, tongue in cheek, to his Algonkian interlocutor, 'for the matters we are now about to discuss are the most important in the world — I am referring, of course, to the great and holy truths of the Christian religion.' 'Dear brother,' answers the Indian, 'if you can make any sense at all out of what the Jesuits try to put down our throats, I'll be very grateful to you. But if you yourself believe what they believe, we may as well call a halt right now. For they've told us such an ill pack of nonsense that I can hardly do them the intellectual insult of believing they believe it all themselves . . .'

So, for an eighteenth-century mind, questioning Western assumptions (well, some of them), the Indian is a 'naked philosopher' who helps him to see things in a radical light. For a nineteenth century mind, wrapped in bovine complacency, the Indian is a 'poor child' whose only chance is to get converted as soon as he can before conking out. What is he for us today, at this end of another century? A nostalgia. The memory of one of the most beautiful cultures in the world.

When I leave the Hunter's Rest the next day, early, ready to take the first bus for anywhere, it's to plunge, breathing freely again, into a beautiful frostblue and rosyfingered morning. A slightly weird note is introduced into this scene when the police car, the big-shouldered, flat-eyed car of the *Sûreté Municipale*, heaves into sight at the end of Main Street and noses its way along, slowly and surely, like the snake in paradise.

Boy, am I glad to be leaving Dolbeau!

The 6.30 bus doesn't stop at Pointe-Bleue, it makes a beeline for Quebec. There's a bus for Roberval at 7.30.

That will be fine and dandy.

I make for a place to eat.

Light meals. Amusements.

'One egg sunny side, toast 'n' coffee.'

I'm sitting just next to two great big fat Pepsi and Coke machines. To my right, a poster advertising the *Concours de Panache* (Antler Competition) of the Dolbeau Hunters' Club. To my left, a poster for Supercool Fruitflavoured Slush.

And the neon light is burning in the tabernacle.

I have a little talk with John Cowper Powys ('If I have learned anything from my life in America, it is a certain lonely and perhaps desperate stoicism.'), then make my way back to the bus station.

Frost on the maple leaves that litter the ground.

A radio announces 'a touch of cold on the heights'.

The bus engine begins to throb and fume.

Roberval.

What's that statue right in the middle of town?

HOMMAGE A SAINT JEAN DE BREBEUF ET A SES COMPAGNONS MARTYRS

That's the guy they must have named the lake after.

Another Jesuit, I suppose.

OK, so the Indians did him in.

Good for them.

Of course, they shouldn't have actually *killed* him. That was bad tactics. They should just have *laughed* him out of the way, or dipped him in the lake. But he probably goaded them into it. I can see the scene from here.

'Dearest Indians,' says this ghoul-haunted goon, advancing under cover of a big brass cross, 'dearest and most cherished brethren, I am here to tell you how to gain Eternal Life. I know you are going to martyr me, of course, but before you martyr me, I want to tell you about the Good Lord and Eternal Life. Incidentally, I've got a little sausage in my pocket, you likee?'

'Will someone please remove that paranoiac pervert?'

'Ah, sticks and stones . . .'

'Give him the shove, will you?'

'Ah, ah, I know you're going to martyr me . . .'

'Nobody's going to martyr you, rat-face, we're just giving you the brush-off.'

'You're not going to martyr me? You mean to say I swallow all that crap for years, I come all the way over here to this Godforsaken hole, and you say you're not going to martyr me! You *got* to martyr me!'

'OK, rat-face, if it's part of your religion, just stop yelling and tell us how to go about it.'

'You take that there cross in your mits and you belt me over the head with it. Right?'

'Right.'

'Well then, go, for Chris' sake.'

They go.

Bam!

'Okay?'

Groan.

One more martyr.

And the Indian goes about forever after with a bad conscience. For centuries they'll be telling him how he did in all those pure-hearted, do-goody priests. He ends up believing it. No wonder he takes to the bottle.

Crows and starlings are flying over Roberval as I set out on the road to Pointe-Bleue, and there's a fresh breeze blowing.

KUEI
IL- NU- TENI
Welcome
Indian Village
Founded 1856. Pop. 1587
Montagnais Tribe

So, here we are at the Pointe-Bleue reservation. I make for the community centre.

There I learn that the chief is on holiday in Switzerland and that his second is away hunting at Chibougamou. That's OK, no problem. It's not chiefs I really want to see, it's shamans. And I may have to make do with ghost shamans. I know that.

Seeing there's a museum in the community centre, I go through it, picking up a little information about the Montagnais territory, Indian hunting techniques, and how to tan caribou hides. I'm a glutton for knowledge. Even if I never have to tan a caribou hide in my life, I know how to go about it. You wouldn't have a little bit of bear grease on you, would you?

After the museum, I explore the village. It's in a craft shop, just a bit beyond the Hudson's Bay Store, that I meet John Robertson. Robertson has 'Indian status'. His grandfather came from Glasgow to work for the Hudson's Bay Company, married an Indian woman and went Indian. 'It's a real pleasure to meet another Scotsman,' he says, in French ('*Ça me fait rudement plaisir de rencontrer un autre Ecossais*').

When I tell John Robertson I'm heading North, he starts talking about the Naskapi. According to him, they're a mixture of Indian and Inuit, i.e. Eskimo. Says I'll run across them at Scheffer (Schefferville). They were sent down there from Fort Chimo, after starving for years on end, ever since the caribou deserted that part of the country. And where did the caribou go? Who knows (*mystère*)? But the Naskapi, they're at Schefferville. Some others maybe at North West River, but he's not sure.

In another shop, a little bar, I meet the son of the house, a tall, solid-built fellow with long black hair, who wants to become a trapper. He's going to attend a hunting school, up in the woods behind Dolbeau. Yes, he likes the idea of going after the animals. He'll scoot about in a skidoo and concentrate on lynx — 'they pay best'.

We're talking about all this when the old granpappy comes down: eighty-five years old, and was in the woods every year till he was seventy. He throws a glance at my rucksack:

'You a traveller? Must be fun, travellin'.'

I say he must have travelled a lot in his time.

'Nah, bein' in the woods, that ain't travellin'.'

'So, what's travellin'?'

'Takin' the plane, seein' foreign places, that's travellin'.'

'You want to see foreign places?'

'I wanta see foreign women.'

By this time the mother has joined us, and we have three

generations together.

The mother remarks on the chilliness of the weather: '*Il ne fait pas une belle température.*' It was snowing yesterday, and they've all got colds. 'We're not tough anymore.' It's the food, she says. She buys an eight-pound chicken at the store, but it dwindles down to four pounds while you look at it. All water. Full of chemicals too. No good. And they don't take enough exercise. Don't move around the way they used to. Always huddled around the television. 'You're more Indian than we are.'

I'm leaving Pointe-Bleue on the way back to Roberval when I hear a scuffling and a giggling at my back.

Three little girls, about twelve years old.

I ask them what they think of Pointe-Bleue.

'It's great.' ('*C'est le fun.*')

More giggling, and talk in Montagnais, while they keep at my heels.

'How do you say "so long" in Montagnais?'

More giggles.

'*Niaut.*'

'Well, *niaut*!'

'*Niaut*!'

It really was getting colder, and the sky was grey. The sun up there like a tiny dime.

I move around
I move around

the limits of the earth
the limits of the earth

I've got wings and I fly
I've got wings and I fly

That's a ghost dance song. Couldn't get it out of my mind.

ESKIMO JOE

After the road, the trees . . . After the trees, unknown territory . . . After that, nothing at all.

Louis-Ferdinand Céline

The next stage meant the bus for Seven Islands, up the North Coast, passing through Sainte-Rose-du-Nord, Sacré-Coeur-Saguenay, Tadoussac, Grandes-Bergeronnes, Sault-au-Mouton, Betsiamites, Baie-Comeau, Godbout, Baie-Trinité, Pointe-aux-Anglais, Rivière-Pentecôte, Port-Cartier, Clarke City . . .

We've been lapping up mile after mile in the clear blue light of an October afternoon. There were a few passengers when we left Chicoutimi, but the bus emptied at Tadoussac, and now there's only myself and a hunter in a woollen tartan shirt with rucksack and rifle.

Walt Whitman visited the 'savage Saguenay country' around 1880. Wrote a little piece about it, saying that the Saguenay is different from all other rivers: 'a more vehement play of light and shade'. He was intrigued too, old Walt, by the echoes at Tadoussac (*taj-oo-sac*, he adds in brackets, to make sure we get the French-Canadian pronunciation right), and admired capes Eternity and Trinity: 'They have impressed me more profoundly than anything of the kind I have yet seen.'

The hunter got off at Les Escoumins and made off into the red woods. It looked as if I was going to be all on my own. But a couple of Indians came on at Betsiamites.

'Payin' your cousins a little visit?' says the driver, used to seeing the Betsiamite Indians travel up to the Seven Islands reservation to say hello to their friends.

'Sure thing.'

The Indians settle down and break open a pack of beer.

The coast is very beautiful.
Rocks, gulls — and there, blue-grey, a heron!
COD FOR SALE.
Crows perched on fir trees.
FRESH SALMON.
Night falls around 5.30.
We pass an aluminium plant lit up like a Christmas tree.
A few miles farther on, Seven Islands.
I get off with the Indians and plunge into the darkness.

It's later that night I make the acquaintance of Eskimo Joe.

He's planted there on the sidewalk, swaying back and forth, back and forth, and spouting a garrulous monologue into the heathen darkness.

A King Lear of the ice!

When I get close to him, he thrusts his face, framed in the furred hood of an anorak, into mine and says:

'Spare a quarter?'

I ask him what for, but the question is rhetorical, for the smell off his breath would make a whale turn pale.

'Rum!'

I put my hand in my pocket. What comes out is a dollar. I hand it over.

'Come on and have a drink!'

He shouts that with an accent as Irish as the pigs of Docherty.

Who is this guy? A Killarney Eskimo? The playboy of the Northern world?

We go into the bar.

The barman looks at the Eskimo, and he looks at me, but he doesn't say anything.

'Rum! Two!'

The rum is on the counter.

Bottoms up.

'Where're you from?'

'Nain! North Labrador!'

I ask him his name.

'Just call me Joe. That's what they always call me . . .'

And he goes into a long mumbling monologue about 'they'.

I'm curious to know more.

'You work here?'

'No, man, I'm *out* of work here!'

'What did you do?'

'Iron Ore! The Company!'

And he goes back into his stumbling monologue.

'Where'd you get that Irish accent?'

'All over the place! Construction gangs! I cover the world!'

'Where are you going now?'

At that last question, a wild gleam comes into his hyperborean eyes and with a majestic sweep of his arm, he thunders:

'Trans-Canada!'

WHITE NIGHT

Through caverns measureless to man,
down to a sunless sea.

Sam T. Coleridge

Midnight, on the North Coast.

Standing at the window of my room, watching a cold mist rolling slowly over the St Lawrence.

Recalling certain transcendental travellers of my acquaintance . . .

Speaking of the poem that haunted him, like some nebula in his mind, Samuel Taylor Coleridge, that Kubla Khan of the intelligence, said that it would be inconceivable for him to devote less than twenty years to it: ten years to bring the materials together (with readings in mechanics, hydrostatics, optics, astronomy, botany, metallurgy, fossilism, geology, chemistry, anatomy, medicine and the psychology of man as revealed in voyages and chronicles), followed again by five years in which to let all that material settle, followed again by five years for the actual composition of the poem.

That was Coleridge's dream as he walked around the lakes of Northern England.

Henry Thoreau walked around the shores of Walden Pond. At Walden, Thoreau was a marginal. But on his trip to Mt Ktaadn, he's even more radical than that. There, he's no longer in the margin, he's *turning a page*, and a great nihilistic, superhumanist wind is blowing:

'It is difficult to conceive of a region uninhabited by man. We habitually presume his presence and influence everywhere. And yet we have not seen pure Nature unless we have seen her thus vast and drear and inhuman . . . Nature was here something savage and awful, though beautiful. I looked with awe at the ground I trod on . . . This was that Earth of which we have heard, made out of Chaos and Old Night. Here was no man's garden, but the unhandselled globe. It was not lawn, nor pasture, nor mead, nor woodland, nor lea, nor arable, nor wasteland. It was the fresh and natural surface of the planet Earth . . . There was clearly felt the presence of a force not bound to be kind to man. It was a place for heathenism and superstitious rites, to be inhabited by men nearer of kin to the rocks and to wild animals . . . Talk of mysteries! Think of our life in Nature, daily to be shown matter, to come in contact with it: rocks, trees, wind on our cheeks — the solid earth, the actual world! Who are we? Where are we?'

'We are Hyperboreans,' says Nietzsche, 'we are well aware in what remoteness we live. "Neither by land or by sea will you find the way to the Hyperboreans" — already Pindar knew that . . . We alone have found the way out of millenia of labyrinth . . . We were sick of modernity. Rather live in the icelands than among all that mush, all that "tolerance" . . . For long we looked for a way, in vain. Our natures darkened, there was a storm in our air. We wanted lightning . . . They called us fatalists. But our fate was a gathering of forces.'

Herman Melville came North to Canada on his honeymoon trip, when he was twenty-nine years old. In Montreal, he met Captain Coffin, about to leave on a whaling expedition up the North Coast to Labrador. Maybe that was when the idea of the White Whale started germinating. There was a girl in it too, way back in Melville's fertile and chaotic mind. A girl he met in the course of his British trip, on the stage-coach between London and Bristol. Her name? Adelina White.

A few months back, at Stromness, a little port in the Orkneys where the whalers used to take on crew before going up farther North, I was in the local museum, admiring a collection of harpoons: the elegant lines, the dull glint on the points.

I was admiring the harpoons, thinking of Melville — and of a word I'd woken up with in my mind that morning, with no memory at all from what context it had sprung: the word 'archaeography'.

The writing of some archaic, archetypal being?

I'd seen the wild runes carved on the stones at Maeshowe: 'These runes were cut with an Iceland axe by the best poet West of the ocean!'

Melville spoke of 'ontological heroes'.

There's a love of the world in them (as well as a disgust with what humanity makes of it), an immense, an *encyclopaedic* love, and an expense of their own persons that can amount to an ecstatic annihilation.

Is the thing to build up an Atlantean library, somewhere on the edge of things, as a focal point above all the twaddle? Or else, beyond all libraries, to try and put one's finger on the pulse of our living earth, giving voice, however fragmentary, to the primal world?

Probably both.

In order to arrive, somewhere, at something beyond all the family albums.

'Nobody ever goes North, to the extreme North of human being,' says Valéry.

Thoreau thought he'd have to become Indian.

Hardy said the new Tempe would be somewhere around Thule.

'Trans-Canada,' said Eskimo Joe.

I translate: 'Trans-humanity.'

Here in my room, on the high North Coast of being . . .

Before calling it a night, I take the half-bottle of whisky from my rucksack and drink to all ontological heroes everywhere.

THE WIND AT SEVEN ISLANDS

Never have I felt so strongly my detachment from myself and my presence in the world.

Albert Camus

In the morning, I'm standing at the Old Pier of Seven Islands, looking out over the big blue white-flecked river and thinking of Jacques Cartier, whose *Travels of Discovery in Canada* have been with me ever since I left France:

'On the Thursday we came upon seven high islands . . .'

That was 19th August, 1535.

Four and a half centuries later, the same seven islands are still there to see: the Big Basque and the Little Basque, the Corossol, the Big Boule and the Little Boule, Manowin and the Ile Dequen, bathed in the rosy haze of a St Lawrence dawn. As for the town that grew up on the coast, it's no longer the little Indian settlement it was, frequented by caribou hunters and, later, a handful of Hudson's Bay men. A few years ago, it boomed and it spread, and now it's known the world over as the Iron Klondyke.

Long trains bring the ore down from the mines in West Labrador and it's loaded here on to the ships that carry it farther: to Cleveland, Philadelphia, Rotterdam, Nagasaki . . . One of those big-bellied ships, the *Masukawa Maru*, is lying out there now, massive and silent, off the brand new harbour East of the Old Pier.

But to leave aside the Iron Rush for the moment and come back to Jacques Cartier:

'A brief account of the voyage made to the islands of Canada, Hochelage and Saguenay, with a description of the customs, language and ceremonies of the inhabitants.'

The edition I have of Cartier's *Travels* came out in Paris in 1968. Which is an interesting coincidence. For a good many people in France at that time wanted to see the end of a certain culture and were feeling out for the beginnings of *something else*. That 'something else' has still to be discovered, but it seems to me that it will mean among other things a move from history to geography. Which is why in the Autumn of '68 I got down to reading and re-reading all the old travel-books I could get my hands on.

I loved the sense of freshness they gave me, the rhythm, the direct simplicity. What a relief after all the verbose militancy, all the querulous ideology, all that flat-footed moral-political discourse that kept going round and round the same dreary topics and had *no sense of world* at all. We were suffering from cultural claustration, and that kind of stuff was no cure, it was part of the disease. We needed something a lot farther out.

When Cartier sailed out from St Malo in April 1534, at the age of forty-three, his mission was to find a North-West passage to China, the kingdom of the Great Khan, and bring back to France quantities of precious metals and spices. He found neither the passage, nor the precious metals and spices, but what he did find, in the 'new found lands' were all kinds of birds: swans, cranes, bustards, geese; fish in abundance: mackerel, mullets, bass and big eels; and a strange and wonderful sort of dolphin: 'A kind of fish no man has ever seen or heard of. They have the body and the head of a greyhound and are as white as snow, without a single spot. There are a very great number of them in that river, living between the salt and the sweet water. The local people call them *adhothuys*.'

Cartier may have been a bit put off by the savage and inhospitable landscape of the Labrador coast. But the old retired captain in St Malo, surrounded by family squabbles, must have recalled it with affection. And those dolphins must have glided often enough through his imagination — those sensual dolphins, the beautiful American thing, sporting in the waters of the St Lawrence, which wasn't yet the St Lawrence, just 'the big river'.

A big river full of fish.

A wee fishing smack has been drawing in to the Old Pier, tossing jauntily in the crisp blue waters. I watch it unloading cod, turbot, and crabs.

Leaving the pier, I walk along the waterfront, passing by the Hudson's Bay Store, till, at the corner of Arnaud and Blanche, I come up against the entrance to the Iron Ore Terminal: 'No admittance except on business.'

My business, if you can call it that, being elsewhere, I continue on my way.

When, a couple of hundred yards further on, a taxi passes, I hail it, and we make for the centre of town. I bring up the question of iron ore:

'Here, it's no ore, no life.'

I say I've heard there's quite a lot of unemployment.

'Quite a lot, yeah.'

'How's that?'

'No construction. We've got a bunch of bums in the government.'

'You from Seven Islands?'

'I been here a while.'

'Would you say you were a Seven-Islander?'

'Nope, and I don't know many who would. It isn't a place like that.'

What kind of a place was it? Looking out of the window, I saw thoroughfares, trim villas, gardens with rowan trees . . .

'If you had to describe Seven Islands in one word, what would you say?'

'Empty.'

On the Place de Ville, I go into a shop, ostensibly to buy a postcard. A woman comes to serve me.

'What do people do in Seven Islands?'

'Business.'

'What kind of business?'

'All kinds. Everything goes. You can get what you like.'

Among other wares, this woman sold a rubber Love Doll — 'a life-like companion' — for lonely nights in the work camps.

In the middle of the Place de Ville, there's a big commercial complex. It's like a little city on its own, with spacious alleys, and it's warm in there. When the winds are howling down from the Labrador and the temperature's way below zero, the citizens can walk and shop there in comfort. In fact, you can spend a day in there, for there are cafés and restaurants too.

I even found a bookshop.

NORTH COAST BOOKSHOP.

What a name for a bookshop!

You imagine it full of books to find the true North again, books of mental navigation, books crammed with physical metaphysics and poetic cartography.

The two young women who run it tell they have a hard time: 'Culture is thin on the ground here.' Although they try to stock books with some mental energy in them, books that reveal the world, that augment the sensation of life, what they're mostly asked for are school texts, and books on occultism, with the usual dose of novelish novels.

I go along the shelves.

One title intrigues me.

Le Passage du Nord-Ouest.

I flip through the pages. The kind of chaos-cosmic thinking and exploring I like.

I buy it and retire to a café to read it.

What a jolt that was!

Right from the preface, the author, Michel Serres, was talking my language. He was even using identical words. Dammit, I could almost recognize my portrait:

'The new Zeno, from Paris and London, called his method a "random" method, thinking of the old French word *random*, a hunting term, which was to give rise to two cognate words: the French *randonnée*, meaning excursion, and the English *random*, chance or hazard. His aim was to bring the two senses together, crossing the channel, or the St Lawrence . . .'

Holy smoke!

For years, taking myself basically for an 'extravagant Scot', I'd been talking about 'intellectual nomadism', while living 'at random'. I'd crossed the Channel, burning my boats, and I'd moved through Paris and Amsterdam, and Barcelona, and Tunis, and Bangkok, and Taipei . . . and now here I was, at large, on the North Bank of the St Lawrence. I read on:

'A white space, where there are no stakes and nothing to fight against . . . a difficult connection . . . a crossing of the desert . . . a new archipelago . . . a narrow and infrequent passage . . . reality throws out complex signs, whereas all dualism is polemical, and new thought dies there . . . if he's to survive, he has to invent, and he has to invent an absolutely new space that has nothing in common with the accustomed one and its imbecile allotments . . .'

Unbelievable!

I felt like underlining every phrase.

With me the concepts were pelagian thought, archipelagic activity and white world. And here was this guy, starting out from entirely different bases and premises, arriving in the self same area.

Was a new wind blowing over the world?

I was so excited I couldn't stay sitting in the café any longer. I had to get out in the wind and walk.

I walked right across Seven Islands, with the rowan trees waving their red branches all along the way, and arrived back at the Old Pier.

The fugitive image of the old pier in a certain village on the West coast of Scotland crossed my mind. And I thought of those citizens of New York Melville talks about, coming down to the piers on Sundays to get a whiff of some larger life. The pier, one of those privileged spots where life is gathered and extended, takes on other dimensions.

Piers, promontories, headlands.

I stood out at the end of the pier watching the gulls.

The white dance!

'What is chaoticism, Mr White?'

That need for words that energize and space out.

The leap into another logic.

Eroto-cosmology.

I was drunk with the wind. Drunk with the great white rumour of the St Lawrence. Drunk with ideas.

Ideas like fish and gulls.

Swimming thinking, winged thinking.

Oceanic philosophy.

Why write? So as not to go completely crazy with that kind of drunkenness. That white drunkenness that is the source of all real writing.

As I made my way back to my room in the North Coast Hôtel, I passed a girl selling apples from a cart.

She had the bluest eyes I've ever seen.

In those eyes I saw Labrador.

ON THE COAST

Here, we are prisoners of war. But there is another world.

Black Elk

The St Lawrence shone bright green that morning, and there was a bite of frost in the air. You could imagine sleek beavers busy in the streams and herds of caribou padding out their paths on the high plateau.

I was walking along Brochu to the reservation.

A time was when they were scattered all over North-Eastern America, following the caribou trails, trapping beaver. They called themselves, in the Algonkian tongue, *Innut*, 'the human beings'. When the French explorers arrived in the Gulf of the St Lawrence in the sixteenth century, they called them Montagnais, the mountain-men.

In Summer they stayed on the coast, for the sake of the cool breezes, but as soon as the leaves spoke September, they made their way up to the Labrador plateau for the hunting season. All might have been well if they'd been able to keep moving from coast to plateau, from plateau to coast, according to the rhythm they knew. But the missionaries were against it — for a wanderer, as those harpies well knew, is not so easily converted as a settled person: 'We can't expect much from the Savages so long as they remain nomad . . . Whereas nations with a fixed abode might be converted without great difficulty' (the Jesuit Lejeune, 1634). Break the life-rhythm, break the mind. Get a mind with no life-rhythm at all, it'll believe anything.

When shops started up in the same places as the missions, the Innut were sedentarised, and that was the beginning of the end. History's final place for them was the reservation where the 'savage' could nurse his neolithic nostalgia, live out his contradictions and confess his newfound sins: '*Konfiteor Teo omnipotenti, Peate Marie semper Pirjini, Peate Mikaeli Arkangelo, Peato Joani Patiste, Sanktis Apostolis Petro et Polo, omnipus Sanktis et Tipi Pater, cuia pakapi nimis kogitatio perpo et opere, mea kulpa, mea kulpa, mea maksima kulpa . . .*'

The Seven Islands reservation is a huddle of shacks built on the sandy shore of the river. A little wind has sprung up and wisps of sand are whispering across the street. It's like a ghost town.

A bleached tree-trunk, part of the river flotsam, has been set up as a kind of totem. It would be easy to see in it the symbol of a dead culture. Yet it gives out a strange power.

Passing by the totem, I see an Indian Handicrafts shop, but the door's closed and there seems to be nobody at home. Maybe it's too early in the day or too late in the season. I take a look in through the little window and when my eyes get used to the gloom I make out two posters. One is the well-known portrait of Red Cloud, with the phrase: 'The earth and I are of one mind.' The other shows a crucifixion scene and bears the motto: *Tous unis en Jésus* (all united in Jesus).

I continue walking along the line of shacks till I come to another *Artisanat Indien*. This one's open. And it's here I meet Thibaut Latuile.

He's about forty years old, Thibaut, short and sturdy, running a bit to fat, with a round, laughing face. When I come in, he's working at a pair of mocassins, and the air of the shack is thick with the smell of tanned hide: a fine, rich, acrid smell, like smoke and honey mixed. And the mocassins themselves are beautiful, the caribou skin a pale yellow with cloudy masses of brown. No, Indians themselves don't wear mocassins anymore, they wear tennis shoes. But he sells a lot during the summer, to Americans and French people mainly. The last French tourists passed through just about ten days ago, a young couple. They had some pot on them and he'd gone down to the shore with them to smoke. The Indians smoke a lot, he adds. He loves it, but they say it makes you lose your memory, it destroys the cells of the brain. He makes nice little pipes for smoking pot — would I like one? No, he's never been on the hard stuff, not like some. Though one time, down in Bersimis, his home village, his best pal (*'mon chum'*) slipped some speed in his beer. That was awful, he felt swollen up twice his size — 'like a mountain'. Really bad deal, that, never again. Yes, he was born down there in Bersimis. Came up here because he thought there'd be more work. He's educated, went to school up to the eleventh grade, and a Bersimis Indian is smarter than a Seven Islands Indian any day. He got a job up in Schefferville, with the Iron Ore. Was signed on as a storeman, because of his education. But when he turned up for the job, the foreman says: 'OK, grab that shovel' (*'pogne la pelle'*). He says: 'No', just like that. The foreman, he says: 'Who's the foreman here?' Thibaut he says: 'Who got signed on as storeman?' He finally got his rights, but pretty soon he got bored, so he threw in his chips and came back down to Seven Islands and opened a handicrafts shop: his own boss, except for his wife (she decorates the mocassins) . . . He's interested in Indian affairs, would like to get on the tribal council (*conseil de bande*). He went to a Council meeting once, to get things off his chest. They listened to him, 'with their cheeks in their hands'. When he'd finished, they said that must have done him good to talk. He said he hadn't come to make a record (*'Mouei, j'ai dit, je ne suis pas venu itsi pour faire un disque'*) . . . He's against the separation of Quebec. The federal agent is his chum, they drink beer together, and one day he said to him: 'You're no smarter than I am.' He likes talking, that's true (*'j'aime deviser'*), he likes arguing things out . . . Yes, he's Christian — a faithful Catholic. But he doesn't like what they've done to the mass. The way it was before, he really felt moved (*'ça m'exaltait'*), and he was often near to crying. But the new stuff, it has no effect on him at all. While it's going on, he finds himself thinking of some woman, and it's never the Virgin Mary. Talking of women, maybe I'd like to come over the road and meet the wife?

The house is only a few yards away across the sand. In front of the door, a black dog lies curled up, licking its paws in evident saisfaction. Thibaud gives it a pat on the head: 'He's a smart one.' (*'Il est smat.'*)

Along with Thibaut's wife, there are two young children in the house, and their elder daughter, with her husband. Wife, daughter, son-in-law, children, like Thibaut himself, are waxing fat. He remarks on that: 'We're all fat — it's the sedentary life.' And the children are spoiled, they're always guzzling at ice-cream and coca-cola. 'And *you're* always guzzling at beer,' says his wife, laughing, as Thibaut tugs open the fridge. It's true, he says ruefully, he used to weigh 130 pounds, now it's 180, too heavy. All comes from boredom, sheer boredom. The Indian was healthier before. There was no cancer or anything then. By the way, he's got Indian remedies for some sicknesses. Did I ever have toothache? He has stuff, you just smear it on the painful tooth, wait five minutes, and, hey presto, the tooth *cracks*, and you can just pick it out. And he has one sure fire cure for colds: beaver's balls (*couilles de castor*) . . . A cute little Indian girl passes by. Thibaut goes over to the window to have a better look: '*C'est mon kick*,' he says, '*j'ai un kick pour elle*' ('She's my girl, I'm nuts about her'). His wife laughs, and asks me if I've ever eaten Indian food. I say no. So maybe I'd like some Indian bread (*bannick*) with coffee? She wants to make you as fat as herself, says Thibaut, rejoining the company after a last lingering look at his dream girl. While Madame Lathuile is bringing out the bannock bread, with a pot of jam made of *graines rouges*, and is brewing up the coffee, I talk with the son-in-law and the daughter. It turns out the son-in-law is a Naskapi, born in Fort Chimo, up on the Bay of Ungava — 'among the Eskimo', as his wife says, laughing. 'There's nothing wrong with the Eskimo,' says Thibaut, 'they're better off than we are. They eat raw meat, those fellows, that's why their teeth are so white. They don't eat the crap we eat.' (*'Ils ne mangent pas les saloperies que nous mangeons'*) . . . The son-in-law works for the Iron Ore Company up in Schefferville, but he and his wife are down in Seven Islands to consult a doctor for their little boy. I ask if there are any Indian doctors. 'We're not intelligent enough,' says the daughter. Thibaut doesn't say anything to that. Neither does the son. Madame Latuile brings over the coffee.

I'd left the Latuile house, with promises to visit them again, and was sitting on the shore, at the edge of the reservation, my back against a floated treetrunk, watching the river rolling by, when I heard a rattling of pebbles and someone coughing, and a young man came up:

'Where do you come from?' ('*De quelle place vous êtes?*')

'France.'

'Where in France?'

'The Pyrenees. The big mountains in the South.'

'You're not from Paris?'

'No, I'm not from Paris.'

'It must be fun to live in Paris.'

'You wouldn't like it there.'

'I don't like it here. The reservation's full of jealousy.'

'So is Paris.'

'But Paris isn't the reservation.'

'Well, it's bigger. And they've cut down the woods there.'

'I don't like the woods.'

'Maybe you'd like Paris then.'

'I would love Paris.'

'What do you do around here?'

'I do studies. I'll get a thousand dollars a month.' ('*J'aurai mille pièces par mois.*')

'What kind of studies?'

'Evening classes. To be an accountant.'

'You like accounts?'

'I like a thousand dollars a month.'

'OK.'

'What do *you* do?'

'For the moment I'm just travelling around.'
'That your job?'
'Not exactly.'
'Where you going now?'
'Further up the coast. Then to Goose Bay.'
'A lot of hot women up there.'
'At Goose Bay?'
'Yeah.'
'That's fine. You been there?'
'I heard about it. Me, I've never gone further up than Mingan. My lungs are no good. You like a beer? My name is Jean-Claude Vollant.'

He suggests we go to his cousin's. But before making for there, we pay a little visit to the reservation grocery, where we buy a 'dose', that is, a pack of beer. Jean-Claude tells me it takes five beers for him to feel *paqueté,* to get the *feeling.* What he really likes is to drink beer and then smoke grass — that way, you really *go* (*tu pars*) . . . On the road to his cousin's place, he informs me he doesn't want to get married, he's sterile. Fed up with big families anyway. His father spawned fourteen kids (*il a pas mal craché*), so if he doesn't have any at all, that'll even things up.
'Are you a Catholic?'
'Sure.'
'You all Catholics here?'
'It's a Catholic reservation. The Naskapi, they're Protestant.'
I tell him about the posters in the first handicrafts shop: the one with the phrase 'the earth and I are of one mind,' and the other with the phrase '*tous unis en Jésus.*' I ask him if he doesn't see a contradiction there.
'A contradiction?'
'Well, two different ways of looking at things.'
'What things?'

'Things in general. The way you live and think.'

'Nobody's ever asked me that question.'

'Maybe it isn't a good question?'

'I don't know.'

And then he adds:

'The Indians haven't wakened up yet.'

The cousin was putting the finishing touches to a porcupine quill necklet when we arrived with the beer. With him was another man, also about thirty years old. He'd just come down from the Ungava territory where he'd been doing some surveying. That was his job, surveying.

'What's Ungava like?'

'Don't like it.'

'Too cold?'

'Too cold, that's part of it. No animals — only seals and whales. It's another world.'

We drank the beer and let the ideas come slowly.

The surveyor said he was trying to get the best of both worlds: the Indian's world and the white man's world. As for Bruno, the cousin, what he liked was to go hunting. He'd take the Schefferville train and go up inland for about a hundred miles and get himself a caribou. He told about an old hunter in the reservation who up to a couple of years ago spent half the year up there on his own. He'd still be at it, only didn't walk too good any more. ('*Il a une misère à marcher maintenant.*')

Jean-Claude put a record on the pick-up:

'Indian folk rock. You like it?'

'Yes, I like it. What's it called?'

'*Mashte chipu.* Big River.'

'Where's it come from?'

'Here.' ('*Itsi.*')

'Who's the composer?'

'Philippe Mackenzie. He's a cousin of the people that run the shop you saw the posters in.'

When I finally took my leave, I made for the shop with the posters.

There was somebody in there this time: a young woman. She was sorting out beaver skins, really beautiful skins, thick and lustrous, dark brown at the centre, ruddy gold at the rim.

'Beautiful skins.'

'Very beautiful.'

'I'd like to buy one.'

'Take your pick.'

I took my time choosing the one I wanted.

'Still a lot of trapping done around here?'

'Still some. Despite everything.'

'What's everything?'

That really set her going, Rose-Marie Fontaine. It all came out *pêle-mêle*, as though she'd just been waiting for a chance to spill it.

She told me about a river: the River Moisie. When her father wanted to hunt now, when he wanted to go to his traditional hunting grounds, he had to have a pocketful of permits signed by one office after another. And there were some places he just couldn't get a permit for, like the River Moisie, where 'our ancestors' had always fished for salmon. He couldn't get a permit because a Club had taken over the river. What right had a Club to take over a river? Did they know what salmon meant to the Indian? Of course they didn't. Her father knew all about salmon, he'd told her all the stories about salmon, but he wasn't allowed to fish the salmon any more, only rich Americans and Canadians could do that. A while back, she'd been to the river with her father and her uncle, and there'd been a fight, a tongue fight, though some shots were fired too. But the Club was still there and there were more of them to come . . . Since she was a very young girl, she'd spent four months of every year with her father in the woods. She loved that. She loved living in the tent. People say the Indians are dirty and slovenly. That's because they're not living in their own way. When they live in the tent, they're clean. Every day they change the floor, laying fresh, sweet-smelling branches. Houses are all right, but they're not Indian. That's why the people don't take care of them. And they don't make little gardens, like the white people. If you've got woods, you don't need a garden. The Indian needs the woods. Without the woods, he's not happy, so he gets drunk. You can't blame him for that. The white people don't understand him, even those with good intentions. Sometimes the Indian doesn't understand himself any more. That's it, yes: the Indian doesn't understand himself any more.

I asked her about the contradiction I saw between the two posters on the wall. She said she'd never thought about it. She'd been brought up in the Catholic religion. Only once she'd been against the priest, that was years ago, when they tried to force the folk here to abandon the reservation for another farther away from town. They were trying to make the Indian *invisible*! Her father had refused. The priest, he was on the side of the authorities, and he'd said that if her father didn't move with his family to the new place, a few miles north, at Maliotenam (the village of Mary Immaculate), God would punish him. Her father had stood his ground, and although there were more facilities up at Maliotenam, at least they were still in their own place. She hadn't liked the priests then. But mostly they were good men, and they stood by the Indian, they were like fathers to them. She'd been brought up to think that way. Some of the old Indian ways frightened her. Her uncle could make the dead speak (*'il fait parler les bonshommes qui sont morts'*). He knew old songs too, and he sang them in the woods or at dances, beating on his drum. She liked them, but they worried her a bit too. She liked ordinary French songs better, they didn't give you goose flesh.

I'd pricked up my ears when I heard about the uncle. So there was someone here who still carried on the old shaman ways?

Marie-Rose had noticed my interest. Maybe I'd like to meet her uncle? Well, I could go visit him tonight, when he got back from his job at the Iron Ore Terminal. She'd let him know I was coming. What was my name? I asked her what her uncle's name was. Jean-Baptiste Mackenzie, she said, and she gave me his address.

As I was about to leave, she said she wanted to make me a present. It was a prayer book in Montagnais, bearing the title *Sheshus Nashauatau (Jesus our Saviour).*

While waiting in a little roadside restaurant for the agreed hour, I flipped through the pages of the prayer book. It was illustrated, and there were two types of illustration. On the one hand, purely pious images, such as the Virgin Mary and Child, or a ciborium full of holy wafers. On the other, scenes of Indian life: a hunter with rifle in a snowy forest, a river glowing in the sunlight. Everything had been done to make the Indian feel at home in the arms of Jesus, and the Great Manitou himself had been converted, at least on paper:

> *Uin Tsishe Manitu tshi minukunu aiamieu anuenimitishun*
> *Anuenimitishueiku, katshi pastatutamek*
> *Tsishe Manitu tshi ka uantshissistam katshi anuetuk*
> *Tsishe Manitu tshi ka kashimakuau tshi pastaitunuau . . .*

JEAN-BAPTISTE

The whole effort of man was to get his life into contact with the elemental life of the cosmos: mountain-life, cloud-life, thunder-life, air-life, earth-life, sun-life.
D. H. Lawrence

It was a young fellow with a tall black hat came to the door.

'Is this the house of Jean-Baptiste Mackenzie?'

'Yes. Mr Kenneth White?'

'That's right.'

'Come on in.'

Quite a few people were gathered in the room the black-hatted one lead me into. There was Jean-Baptiste himself, a handsome man about sixty years old,. his wife, a good-looking woman about the same age, and two strapping sons: the one with the hat, and another with long black hair reaching to his shoulders — they both looked a lot more Indian than their parents. There was also the wife of one of the sons, very good-looking too, and a little boy about twelve years old, a more or less distant relative.

The little boy's father had just been killed on a hunting trip. He and some friends had hired a plane to take them up into the territory between Schefferville and old Fort Mackenzie, along the banks of the River Caniapiscau. It had been good hunting and the boy had shot his first caribou, a female, and the young one in its grief kept turning around the dead body: '*Il a une misère, il fait rien que tourner autour.*' It was on the way back that the plane crashed, into a lake, and there were only two survivors, the boy and the pilot. Jean-Baptiste told the story, with the boy listening calmly, adding only that one phrase: 'He was suffering, he kept turning round the dead body.'

Jean-Baptiste recalls how he used to go from Seven Islands to Schefferville on foot. Days and days and days it took him, and he enjoyed every minute of it: '*Kolis, c'était une vie, ça!*' ('Dammit, that was a real life!') Whereas now the mining companies are reducing the hills to dust and piling it up at Seven Islands and the mills are turning the forests into pulp, and the big dams are drying up all the rivers. Yes, it was better before, in the woods you could really live (*c'était mieux avant, dans le bois, c'est une vie*). You can't hunt and fish any more the way you used to because of the Company's pollution (*à cause de la pollution de la Compagnie*). In ten years, Seven Islands will be as big as Montreal, and there'll be no life at all, just business. Or maybe there won't even be business, because once the companies have got what they want, they'll drop everything: '*Salut, Marcel.*' Once they've filled their pockets, they'll be off, and there'll be nothing left here but a dreary wasteland.

I ask the black-hatted one what he thinks of that. He looks embarrassed, then he says:

'He likes to talk. But he's maybe right.'

'You want to hear the songs?' says Jean-Baptiste.

'Yes, if you don't mind.'

'I don't mind. Let's go down to the cellar.'

So we go down to the cellar.

Jean-Baptiste tells me he works for the Company from eight till four, then he works for himself, down here in his cellar, doing handicrafts. He's got a work bench with a lathe. There are various bits and pieces of bone on the bench. I pick up what looks like a shoulder bone:

'Caribou.'

He says he's getting ready for a hunting and fishing trip now, shows his tent of Hudson Bay cloth and the new sinkers he's made for his lines. The rifles hanging from nails are a .28 that belonged to his father and a .22 his father gave him when he was a boy. He says you can kill a caribou with a .22. But nowadays there are more elks going about than caribou. The caribou are mysterious. They come and go, nobody knows why or where.

His drum is lying on another table. He'd been cleaning it just before I arrived. He cleans it once a year, because 'if the drum isn't ready, you can't sing'. ('*quand le tambour n'est pas prêt, on ne peut pas chanter*'.) He picks it up and begins to talk about it. The white skin of the drum is caribou, and the wooden rim, painted red, is of birch wood. Across the surface of the drum is stretched a line of quills, to give a rattling sound. These are the quills of the white partridge, though you can also use the quills of wild duck, or even small caribou bones.

He tunes the drum.

When he's in the woods, he says, he beats on the drum to call the caribou. And as he tells me about it, his phrasing seems to become more rhythmical, like this:

When you go up into the woods
when you're up there in the woods
you consult the drum
you use it like a TV set
you see what you're going to kill
when you hunt with the drum . . .

Would I like a cassette of his songs? He has a portable recorder on his bench, a dilapidated little thing held together by Scotch tape. He says he likes to record things for his children. Especially when he's *en voyage*, travelling. He's made recordings for them of the sound of his paddle on the lake, and the sounds of his steps on the snow of the forest, and of his songs too, of course, because soon they won't know all that and he doesn't want them to forget everything, memory's important. He's fifty-eight years old, and he knows he'll die soon, because he's sick. If he makes a cassette of his songs for me, he knows they'll travel far (*comme ça, mes chants voyageront loin*). People like his songs. When he sings them, the old people cry out: '*C'est vrai, ça, Mackenzie, c'est vrai ce que tu dis*!' ('That's true, Mackenzie, it's true what you say!') The young folk like them too, but they don't know so much, they don't like them for the same reasons. For them, they're just songs. For the old people, they're life.

When Jean-Baptiste beats his drum, he's no longer Jean-Baptiste Mackenzie. He's outside himself, moving in a land that teems with trout and salmon, and on the immense tundra where bands of grunting caribou, thousands of them, migrate from place to place, horns carried high, hooves kicking up the snow or grinding the ice to a fine powder. He sees it all:

They are like ghosts
the caribou
they come and go
they come and go . . .

He speaks of the caribou and he speaks of the leaves in the forest:

I understood the leaves
by the leafy sounds they made
it was Winter and Summer where I walked . . .

He speaks of the birds:

Now I'll tell about the birds
how they fly in bands
going down to the sea
I'll tell about the one
who's out there in front
that old greylag
riding on the wind
you watch it one last time
when Autumn comes

And not only does he speak of them, he actually flies with them, flies with them, all the way to their home in the Arctic:

Flying in the air
flying in the air
I'm on my way
I'm on my way

my Eskimo woman
my Eskimo woman
I'll marry you
I'll marry you

at the centre of the earth
at the centre of the earth . . .

I came away from Jean-Baptiste Mackenzie's place that night with a cassette of songs and the shoulder blade of a caribou:

'When we give a present, we say nothing, we let the present talk.'

THE BIG DANCE AT MINGAN

If I can lead you to go back far enough.
Charles Olson

I was making for Havre-Saint-Pierre.

When I told that to the bus-driver, he said:

'It's the end of the road. Can't go any farther than that. It's the end of the road.'

Two Indian youths got on the bus at the same time as myself. They had a basket of beer with them and a big hunk of *viande sauvage* (caribou meat) wrapped in newspaper.

'Going for a picnic?' joked the driver.

'A marriage,' said one of the Indians.

'Going to be some marriage if you drink all that.'

The Indians grinned.

We pulled out.

On the one hand, the forest, on the other, bays full of boulders and gulls.

I picked out on my big map the names of the bays, and the names of the rivers that come rushing down through the forest: Rivière-au-Bouleau, Rivière Manitou, Rivière-au-Tonnerre . . .

Again I had that clean, crisp sensation of the coast. A first place. The raw beauty of it all.

It was late afternoon, and the sky was a cool blue.

The blue of the sky grew darker and darker, till it was night. It was then one of the Indians in the seats just across the way leaned over and said:

'Like a beer?'

I said 'Sure, thanks.'

Ever tried bringing a beer bottle to your mouth in a jolting bus to nowhere? With every jolt you're liable to lose a tooth . . .

'Good beer, huh?'

'Good, yeah.'

'Where you makin' for?'

'Havre-Saint-Pierre.'

'That's the end of the road.'

'So they tell me.'

'Got friends there?'

'Nope.'

'How come you go there then?'

'Maybe just because it's the end of the road.'

Pause to consider.

'You in the reservation yesterday?'

'That's right.'

'Heard about you.'

'I met a lot of people.'

'Excuse me one minute. I need a piss.'

With that, he paddled his way up to the back of the bus and pissed on the floor. I could hear it trickling down the runnel.

'Ever heard of Mingan?' he said, coming back to his seat.

'Saw the name on the map.'

'That's where we're going. Me an' my cousin. He's drunk already. We're goin' to a marriage.'

'I heard that.'

'Wanna come?'

'What'd I do there?'

'Dance an' drink, same as everybody else.'

'OK, thanks, I'll come.'

I didn't know what I was letting myself in for, but I was curious, and I could always go on up to Havre-Saint-Pierre the next day. I know where I want to go, but I'm always willing to be blown off my track.

The Indian gave his companion a dig in the ribs:

'He's comin'.'

'Huh?'

'He's comin'.'

'Good.'

As his laconic sidekick subsided back into sleep, the first Indian turned again to me:

'My name's Mathieu. His is Joseph. What's yours?'

'Ken.'

'Ken. OK. You ever eaten caribou?'

'No.'

'You will tonight. Strong meat. Some say elk is more tender, but caribou is better . . . Gettin' close to Mingan now. You know what Mingan means?'

'No.'

'Wolf.'

There's a notice at the entrance to the Mingan reservation that I can just make out by the light of a lamp:

It is strictly defend for any reason to Pierre and Hugues Cousineau and Richard Maloney to enter the Indian reserve on foot or motor vehicle from 30th October 1974 for ever. By order the Tribal Council of Mingan.

I wonder what those three characters did to be excommunicated thus for all eternity, but I ask no questions.

We make for the house of Joseph's family where we're to eat before going to the dance.

When Joseph's mother comes to the door, I get a shock. Down in Seven Islands, the Indians are dressed and look like everybody else. But here at Mingan, it's different. In a few miles, we've gone back a hundred years.

Imagine you're walking through the halls of the Musée de l'Homme in Paris one quiet afternoon and you stop in front of a glass case labelled 'Montagnais Woman, circa 1850' — and the doll *gives a smile and steps out of the case.* Well, that was Joseph's mother. She had on this funny little squashed bonnet, with sausage ringlets at her ears and a pipe in her mouth. Last time I saw anything like that was in the hills of North Thailand several moons ago. Yes, Meo tribes. At first I don't get the connection, but then it comes to me so forcefully I'm surprised I could forget it: Montagnais, that is Algonkin Indians and Meo tribesmen, it's the same thing. Proto-mongol stock. Only some stuck around Tibet, building monasteries and drinking buttered tea, while others wandered North, and kept wandering (what were they really hunting for?) and finally crossed the Bering Straits (can you hear the wolves howling under that frozen moon, can you hear the ice cracking?) and became American.

Primitive, rock bottom Americans, at one with their dream.

So the Mingan people are *primitive*, with primal movement still in their bones and souls, and a dream flickering in their brains. At least that's how the old people are. The younger ones are beginning to look reasonable. But they've still got that gleam in their eye, that pre-Columbian, antediluvian, Great Manitou gleam in their eye, and *anything* can happen.

The beer was circulating, the *viande sauvage* was sizzling, and the conversation was in full swing. Joseph's elder brother Pierre talking:

'When the rummagers (he says *les fouilleux*, and he's referring to ethnologists, archaeologists, *et al*) . . . When the rummagers turn up here, they rummage and they rummage, and they ask a lot of questions . . . Me, I'm careful, I don't trust 'em . . . The Indian's got to be on his guard . . . We were a little bit exterminated, you know... '

A little bit exterminated!

General George Custer calls out: 'So, ya durty Injun, are y' fuckin' dead at last?' And the Indian sings back: 'A little bit!'

Pierre going on. He's drunk a good deal by now, and he's thinking hard. His eyes are all screwed up, and he's wagging an emphatic finger:

'If the Indians had been a bit more ornery, the Canadians wouldn't be here . . . I often think about that . . . When the Indian starts to think about somethin', he thinks about it, he thinks about it all the time . . .'

So Pierre kept thinking:

'Take huntin', for example . . . That's really something . . . If I started to talk about huntin', we'd still be at it tomorrow morning . . . I'm not a hunter myself, not a real hunter, but I can tell you that huntin' for the Indian is a real *big question* . . .'

The old man in the corner, Joseph's mother's father, seems to have been waiting for his cue. He started talking now, as though to himself:

'Way back then, at Mingan, I wasn't married, and I went up into the woods with my grandfather Joseph. We followed the River Romaine up to the lake called Uauiekamau . . . After my marriage I became a real hunter . . . Long journeys they were, especially the one that took us up to Northwest River . . . You know Lake Atikonak? It's up North of here . . . It took us Mingan people five months to get to Northwest River along the Atikonak and the Winuakapau . . . We left in August and we'd get up there in December . . .'

The old man was following the trails of his memory, and we followed them with him:

'Next mornin', we left for a lake where there were beaver . . . We camped there . . . The men went huntin', some for caribou, some for porcupine . . . We left the river and made for a lake that wasn't very far away . . . That's where I saw the cloud raised by the caribou . . . There must have been an awful lot of 'em, for it was a big smoke cloud . . . I'll tell you somethin' . . . Mingan people never hunted foxes . . . We killed caribou, beaver and mink, but we never touched fox . . . There was a good price for fox, but we never touched it . . . We were all like that, at Mingan . . .'

The old man must have felt he had said his piece, for he stopped talking and began to hum a little tune to himself.

The old woman, his daughter, Joseph's mother, brought out a box containing little things she had made out of beads — mostly what I took to be sun symbols. She picked one up and gave it to me: a circle with a green centre and around it red and yellow segments. I thanked her and, laying the object on the table, admired it.

I asked what the red meant.

'The mornin' sun,' said Mathieu.

'The earth,' said Pierre.

And the yellow?

'The sun,' said Pierre.

'The evenin' sun,' said Mathieu.

And the green?

'The grass,' said Pierre.

The caribou meat was ready.

After the meal, we made ready to leave for the dance.

But before leaving Joseph showed me the room I'd be sleeping in later. His. We might not be coming back together. Once at the dance, it was every man for himself. Joseph looked at me with an embarrassed little laugh:

'You don't mind sleepin' with an Indian?' (*'Ça ne te dérange pas, de coucher avec un Indien?'*)

Outside, under the big American moon, who should we meet but my old friend Thibaut from Seven Islands, drunk as a lord, reeling like a capehorner, calling out when he recognised me:

'*Mon chum! Mon chum!* Come on! I've got a hundred dollars. We going to have some fun! I'm as solid as a caribou!'

I don't think he even knew where he was, Thibaut, but he was absolutely at home in his delirium. I put my arm round his shoulders and we made for the dance hall.

There was a big crowd, milling around to the sounds of a demented disco under the smoky light of two red bulbs.

I'm looking around in the red fog for some nice little Pocahontas when I hear a voice at my side. It's a fat boy who tells me he's a student in social studies and continues:

'I'm slightly drunk. I get drunk four times a year. The worst is at the annual Pow Wow . . .'

He waggles about a bit, kind of dancing on the spot, singing to himself, then:

'You sleeping at Joseph's place? Isn't his mother a darling? I'm crazy about her. I'd like to take her into the woods!'

I'm still looking round for a girl to get into the dance with, but visibility is limited.

Suddenly a fight breaks out on the floor. A man and a woman, going at it hammer and tongs. The dancers give them a little space, but keep moving.

'That's nothing unusual,' says the social studies boy, 'we don't pay any attention.'

It's then that Thibaut of Seven Islands emerges from out the noisy circle, dazed and unsteady, but bottle in hand, shouting out to himself and to the world in general:

'Listen to me, I'm *somebody*. I've worked with the Ministry of Indian Affairs!'

Then focussing, not without some difficulty, on me, he says:

'If you're lookin' for medicines . . .' (*'Si tu as besoin de remèdes . .'*)

At that moment something seems to click in his brain, for he brings a Eureka look onto his face, pats his pocket and making the gesture of smoking, gives me to understand that he has on him a little of the *cheeba cheeba*, the *hootchie kootchie,* the Don Juan Special. OK?, he says. OK, I says. So we go out into the woods and light up.

That's when that old American moon really started shining.

And I saw them, children of Kitche Manitou and the Great Bear, straggling through Beringia forty thousand years ago. Tunchrataïga peoples. Second cousins to the bear, the wolf and the caribou.

Smoking in the cold and ancient woods.

Getting in tune with the new country.

Centuries later, millenia later, Algonkians: Abenakee, Cree,

Delaware, Illinois, Mohican, Massachusetts, Micmac, Naskapi, Ottawa, Ohio, Ojibway, Penobscot, Potawatomie, Fox, Shawnee, Winnebago, Montagnais, covering the territory from Quebec to the Bay of Ungava, and from Great Whale River to Goose Bay, all the great plateau.

Still hunting the lichen-chewing caribou, *rangifer tarandus,* wintering on the heights, then in Summer gathering on the coast for fish-feasts and dances . . .

'OK?'

'OK.'

'OK, chum?'

'OK, chum!'

We go back into the dance hall.

In no time at all, I'm doing the Chicoutimi tango with a baby whale who must weight two hundred pounds if she weighs an ounce.

Pocahontas III.

Thar she blows!

THE END OF THE ROAD

The monk: When the entire body crumbles, something still remains — what is it?
The master: The wind is rising again this morning.

Joshu Shinsai Zenji Goroku

It was freezing cold in the shack.

Joseph came lurching in about an hour after me. He didn't come into the room. I don't know where he went. But there were wretching sounds of vomiting all through the night.

Unable to sleep, I went over in my mind all the cold haiku I could think of:

So chill the water
even the gulls
can't get to sleep

Brr, it's hard to sleep
and if you can't sleep
it's even colder

. . . . . .

I must have dozed off eventually.

When I woke, it was still early morning, but the light at the window grew fast in brightness. I let my eyes travel round the room: cases of empty beer-bottles, a pile of medicine packets, a picture of the Virgin Mary, and a card on which somebody had printed in red ball-point the sentence: *Il faut tourner sa langue sept fois dans sa bouche avant de parler* (turn your tongue in your mouth seven times before talking).

The definitive end . . .

Then, through the window, I saw something very beautiful: raised on hurdles at the edge of the wood, a canoe, with gracefully curving lines, symbol of the past, or maybe an eternal present, speaking of high lakes, rivers and rapids — another world.

I felt the urge to get out on the road again right away, so I pulled on my clothes, scribbled a note of thanks, and was off.

Red sun and frost.

Morning in America.

I'm thinking of Thoreau again:

'Methinks good courage will not flag here on the Atlantic border as long as we are outflanked by the Fur Countries. There is enough in that sound to cheer one under any circumstances. The spruce, the hemlock and the pine will not countenance despair. Methinks some creeds in vestries and churches do forget the hunter wrapped in furs who in the twilight of the Northern night does not give over to follow the seal and walrus over the ice. These men are sick and of diseased imaginations who would toll the world's knell so soon.'

Well, Henry, things have got worse since you were around. If you saw the diseased imaginations on the go at this moment, you wouldn't believe it.

And yet.

The morning wind forever blows:

The Great Morning
winds of long ago
blow through the pine tree

I'd thought I might hitch up to Havre-Saint-Pierre, but there wasn't a soul on the road, not a soul. No matter, it was the beginning of another day, fresh and blue, and I was glad to be out there walking, in the middle of nowhere, on my own, watching those big gulls gliding on the wind:

'It is a great thing to realise that the original world is still there, perfectly clean and pure, many white advancing foams, and only the gulls swinging between the sky and the shore.'

Brother Lawrence again.

I travel with my ghosts . . .

A dog left the porch of the sleeping house where it had been sunning itself and started trotting along the road beside me:

'Hello, dog.'

'Woof, woof.'

I'd have preferred to have been all alone, but that old dog felt like some company and a little walk. So I let him pad along beside me.

I'd been walking for about an hour when a truck passed, and I gave it the sign. It went on, then changed its mind and stopped. I said 'so long' to the dog, ran to catch up the truck, and hopped in.

It was a couple of guys from Havre-Saint-Pierre who'd been out since four o'clock hunting moose along the River St-Jean. They'd had no luck.

'What you doin' out so early on the road?'

'Spent the night in the Indian reservation. There was a wedding.'

'I bet they all got plastered good and proper.'

'Just about it.'

'That's their mentality. That's the way they are.' (*'Ils ont une mentalité à eux autres. Ils sont comme ça.'*)

When they dropped me off at Saint-Pierre, a row or two of whiteboard houses with a little splash of colour here and there, I made for the shore and enjoyed a breakfast of bread and tinned mackerel, thinking of yet another ghost-companion of mine, Matsuo Bashô:

'I've had my face burnt in the warm sun of Kirakata in the Northern provinces,' he says in his *Notes from the Genjû Hermitage,* 'and I've trekked along the rough shores of the Northern Sea . . .'

Bashô's thinking of the journeys he recorded in those marvellous little books *Nozarishi Kikô* (*Records of a Weather-exposed Skeleton*), *Kashimo Kikô* (*A visit to the Kashimo Shrine*), *Oi no Kobumi* (*Records of a Travel-worn Satchel*), *Sarashina Kikô* (*A Visit to Sarashina Village*) and, especially, *Oku no hosomichi* (*The Narrow Road to the Deep North*). And as he sits there in the hermitage at Genjû, he looks over his life.

Although human society weighs on him, he's no out and out hermit, and although he's often thought about it, he's never actually become a monk. If he can define himself at all, it's just as a 'careless man of the hills', living like the winds and the clouds. He's made mistakes in his life, sure, but who knows what's best in the end? Maybe the world is all illusion anyway. Better not think too much about it, just go for a stroll around the lake. Or else climb up the hill behind the house and make yourself a 'monkey's bed'. You do that by laying out some pine branches and spreading a straw mat over the branches. So, why not just lie out on your monkey's bed and enjoy a dreamy snooze:

Enjoying the shadow
of the old pine-trees
in the summer wood

Maybe that's how I'll end up too, just lying back and letting it all float away.

But there's still some way to go.

What kind of way?

Spengler (read way back in the subterranean days of Glasgow) speaks of three ways: the classical way, which is adherence to the present and the near; the romantic way, which has an eye to the farthest horizon; and the Chinese way, which means just wandering aimlessly here and there.

Maybe it's time to find some kind of combination. Maybe we go North, South, East and West in order to find the co-ordinates of some new centre. Maybe we have to try and restore a lost connection, before all the divisions set in.

Maybe.

For the moment I'm on the shore at Havre-Saint-Pierre:

Sitting on the shore
at Havre-Saint-Pierre
eating mackerel from a tin

Autumn morning,
red leaves, yellow leaves
the wind

and I'm writing haiku.

Nobody'll ever praise the haiku enough. We need poems (but are they poems?) that go straight into reality like that. It may not always be great haiku you write, but even not so great they can take an awful weight off your shoulders — all that *personal* load. To write a haiku is to jump outside yourself, it's to forget yourself and get a breath of fresh mental air.

Sitting there on the shore, I write a dozen haiku, about the walk, the morning, the Autumn, the shore, the river:

Wind whistling
over the St Lawrence
the flute with no holes

I lift mine eyes unto the sky:
all those gulls
not even looking for a place to shit

The haiku of the end of the road.

End-of-the-road haiku.

They say in the Zen texts: when you get to the top of the mountain, keep climbing. Which is to say: when you get to the end of the road, keep going.

Last thing I saw in Havre-Saint-Pierre was a little maple tree, blushing autumnly for all it was worth.

THE TRAIN TO SCHEFFERVILLE

My eyes shed light on ancient ways.
Blaise Cendrars

I'd heard stories about them down in Montreal: the mining men.

They tell about the lone prospector who makes a lucky strike, sells out his claim to a big mining company, goes down rich as Croesus to Montreal, barges into a garage, buys himself a great white mega-Cadillac, crashes it, comes back to the garage: 'Gimme another one,' crashes with the second, then goes back up North. Then there's the company man who's just had a tiff with his boss. By way of revenge, or maybe just self-expression, he stomps to the parking lot, gets into his car, revs up the motor and drives the thing ramdamslam into his boss's car. It costs him thousands, but he sure had his moment.

So, there they were, at the Seven Islands station, waiting for the train to drag them back up to Schefferville. They'd been on leave, they'd blown their dough at the poker tables, been on the binge ('*se mettre à la brosse*', they say) and fucked their eyes out. ('*aller à la touffe*'.) Nearly all of them had a twelve pack of beer in their hands, but one thin-faced character in a red anorak sported a flamboyant copy of *Nymphes Nues* (*Naked Nymphs*).

Most of the trains are ore trains. But there are one or two passenger trains as well: on the Saturday night and the Tuesday morning. The Sunday night train is exclusively for Company men, as I learned when I turned up. I'd tried to persuade the train-master to let me on it, and had hung about the platform with the warden keeping an eye on me so I wouldn't hop on behind his back, but they were making no exceptions and there was just no way for me to get on that one. But now it was Tuesday morning, and there was no problem. If I was crazy enough to want to go to Schefferville without *having* to go to Schefferville, that was my pigeon.

So I bought me a ticket for Schefferville and settled down for the journey, reading the Rules and Regulations as listed and placarded in a circular of 24th March, 1976:

It is strictly forbidden to:

1. *Intentionally damage company property.*
2. *Possess, sell or consume an alcoholic beverage, or drug, or be under the influence of same, while travelling on this train.*
3. *Instigate a fight and/or participate in same.*

It sounded as if this train was likely to be a rolling version of Sodom and Gomorrah, with all the bedlam and mayhem of old Glasgow-on-a-Saturday-night thrown in.

OK, let her roll.

I took out my map and checked the names of the stations:

Kémat
Tellier
Saumon
Nieman
Nipisso
Tika
Dorée
Tonkas
Bybee
Premio
Canatiche
Waco
Chico
Lake Dufresne
Mai
Eric
Little
Seahorse
Embar

Pitaga
Oreway
Drylake
Atchouanipi
Ross Bay
Ross Bay Junction
Emeril
Shabo
Talzie
Sawbill
Esker
Livingstone
Cavanagh
Eaden
Menihek
Astray
Redore Junction
Knob Lake Junction . . .

If that list made for slow reading, that's the way it goes. You've got time to look around. No rush on this line.

It was a beautiful Autumn morning, and I had my eyes on the landscape. If all hell had broken loose on the train, I think I'd still have kept my eyes on that landscape.

Jean-Baptiste Mackenzie had told me that the railway more or less followed the old Indian trail between the St Lawrence and the Arctic Ocean. Between the St Lawrence and the Arctic . . . The sense of space those Indians had! A sense which the Canadian, by and large, doesn't have and can hardly imagine. It's only a little over a hundred years ago that all the thousands of square miles of territory that had 'belonged' to the Hudson's Bay Company were added to Quebec, and such an awesome increase in space — as though a country like France were suddenly to find itself with Siberia on its doorstep — hasn't yet entered the local conscience. That's why the whole of the North is still a cold enigma to most Canadians, while to the Amerindian it's full of live realities. I wouldn't want to hammer the analogy, but it's something like poetic space to the normalised mind.

I watch the River Moisie flowing through the forest, reflecting the late Autumn sky. Where the Nipissis joins the Moisie, ah, that shimmering of birch leaves!

All quiet on the train. In this carriage at least. Only a couple of lean and bespectacled Yankees from Chicago who must be railroad men the way they keep on about engines and trains: 'She's a CN engine . . . a No 12,' and a red-faced hunter snoring stentoriously beside a bulky load of equipment.

Now and then a man passes through with a walkie-talkie, looking vaguely for something to comment on. As he comes through this time, he says:

'Two smokies on the East side of the train.'

A 'smokie' is an Indian.

The Indians give a wave as we trundle by, and fade back into the forest.

The little stations all along the line are really very little: no more than a handful of shacks and mobile homes for the permanent way men. The train stops for a few minutes, unloads sacks of potatoes, maybe a crate or two of tinned peaches, a side of beef, then moves on.

Between Lake Dufresne and Embar, you leave the Saguenay district and enter Labrador. It's the 52nd parallel. The forest has thinned out, with all its flourish of Autumn colour. Now it's only stunted pine and muskeg.

To get closer in touch with the landscape and breathe some

fresh air, I go out to the platform between the carriages. It reeks of ammonia. This is where the beer-swillers must come to relieve their bladders. There's a half-door to keep 'em from falling into the lap of nature and they just piss against it. I take a look in at the next carriage: Company men sprawled in a dull stupor or noisily playing cards. All in a thick guff of beer, vomit and stale smoke. I go back to my window.

We've left the Autumn sunlight. It's a white Labrador sun that's shining now among grey cloud, and a wind has sprung up. I watch it blow crisp waves over the grey-blue surface of one lake after another.

There's a long wait at Ross Bay Junction.

And night comes down, with a thin slice of moon.

When we arrive at Schefferville, it's pitch dark and the wind's blowing icily. With no idea if Schefferville is near the station or not, and with no idea of what the place is like, I go to the station office and ask a few questions. Then I start hoofing it, till I come to the Labrador Hôtel.

While I'm waiting at the desk to check in, my ears are filled with the thump-thump-thump of disco from the bar, and in the adjacent restaurant I see a bunch of men at a table littered with beer bottles and hot dogs.

I'm getting used to the kind of room I'm shown: big stains on the carpet and cigarette burns all over the table. What's new this time is that when I open the cupboard I'm greeted by a tin helmet that looks as if it's looking for a head. It won't be mine.

I flip through the pages of the phone book: *Labrador Telephone Company.*

Welcome to the kingdom of Saturn.

THE SHAMAN AND THE LIGHTHOUSE-KEEPER

It belongs to the essence of each occasion of experience that it is concerned with an otherness transcending itself.

Alfred North Whitehead

Schefferville also has its totem: a huge lump of iron gripped between bits of railway line. It's rough, tough and technical.

A raw, red place, Schefferville.

Sure, it now has two hôtels, and rows of bungalows for the Company's men and their families, but it's still a raw, red place. There's red mud and red dust everywhere. The remains of a crude violation.

In the beginning, there was only the great, grey-blue silences of Labrador.

With almost equally silent Indians.

Of course the lynx-eyed Indians must have noticed redder patches of earth here and there. But they were just that: redder patches of earth. Useful maybe for keeping a trail in memory.

Then came Father Babel.

As the good father went about telling the good news to the poor benighted Montagnais, he also kept notebooks in which he set down the details of his travels. With reference to this or that spot, he notes: 'rich in iron', 'red, white, metallic sands'. Not only were those Indians out of line with God, they couldn't see progress when it stared them in the face. Nature with them was a presence, they *corresponded* with it. Nobody had told them they ought to master and possess it. They were about to be informed.

Babel's notebooks come into the hands of his bishop. Well aware of their mineralogical interest, the bishop sends them to the Geology Commission of Canada. They in turn send out the geologist, Law, who roams about Labrador in the years 1892-95 and concludes his investigations with the statement that on that immense plateau there are 'ferriferous formations containing perhaps millions of tons of mineral'.

One mine opened after another — the Ferriman, the Redman,

the Retty, the Star Creek, the Timmins . . . — and the loads thick with hematite, limonite, magnetite, ilmenite, goethite and siderite were exploited for all they were worth. Big holes gaped open in the earth, all colours, from blue to red-ochre to platinum-yellow. Not without a weird beauty.

The Indians, who had just heard about Paradise, didn't know what had hit them. Those people tell them about Paradise and then proceed to blow up the very ground they stand on. But they line up for jobs like everybody else. Paradise on pay day. Old scarecrows like Chief Seattle were left talking to the wind:

'For my people, there is not one single spot on this earth which is not sacred. A pine needle shining, a sandy river, a light mist, all is holy in the eyes and in the memory of my people. The sap that rises in the trees bears within it the memory of the Indians . . . What will there be to life if we can no longer hear the cry of the whipoorwill and the croaking of the frogs round the pond at night? It is the end of life and the beginning of mere survival . . .'

Talking to the wind, old man . . .

As you walk in the streets of Schefferville today, you hear a deep explosion and know that another three thousand tons of rock have just been blasted. Helicopters hover about in the air like giant dragonflies, as a caterpillar lumbers off into the wilds in search of new seams. Dragons, caterpillars. It's a strange kind of insect life you sense here, as if an ant-hill had been knocked over and you look on with wonder and a slight disgust at all the hurry-scurrying.

You have a town, a boom town.

The original tin huts have gone, the communal bunkhouses, and the famous Labrador Pioneers Club that oldtimers tell you about. Families have settled. There's a civic centre, a bathing pool, a school, a library . . . Everything for a happy life. Yes, you can make a lotta dough and enjoy life. That's what the prospectuses say, and it's true. Maybe at moments, but just moments, it may seem an entomological kind of life, and you may feel, especially if you're a woman, that you're going off your rocker with claustrophobia, but there are advantages, no doubt about that. Besides, a psychiatrist is just setting up business, and if you want fresh air, you can always dress up your distress in a ski-suit and go a-slippin' and a-slidin' over the slopes of Old Smokey Mountain that bears it all with an icy grin.

Citizens of Schefferville, the Company loves you, and the Company will care for you. It will be there at the birth and it will be there at the death, from the dawn even unto the going down of the sun.

Boom!

I've been out for a walk, letting all that go through my head. Now I'm in my room in the Labrador Hôtel. To make it a little more congenial, I've pinned my big maps from the *Ministère de l'Energie* and the *Ministère des Terres et Forêts* on the wall. That gives space, and a blue-and-white atmosphere to the place.

What am I up to here?

Hard to put a name on it.

Let's say: geomental meditations.

So I look at my maps, I watch the grey-blue sky through my window, and I write poems — one, for example, about the Great Grey Owl which in Taverner's *Birds of Eastern Canada* is referred to as *Scotiaptex nebulosa*, the shadowy ranger . . .

Work in progress.

A while back I was reading Mishima — not the novels, but that little intellectual autobiography called *Sun and Steel.* He starts off that book like this:

'For some time now I've had the feeling that all kinds of things were gathering in my mind and that an objective art form like the novel simply couldn't handle them. A twenty-year-old poet might be able to do it, but I'm no longer twenty years old, and besides, I've never been a poet. So I've been groping my way to another form better adapted to personal matters of this type, and I've come to a sort of compromise between confession and criticism, an ambiguous manner of expression you might call "confidential criticism". A kind of twilight writing half-way between the dark night of confession and the clear daylight of criticism. The "I" I'll be concerned with won't be that of my strictly personal history, but something else . . . Reflecting on the nature of this other self, I came to the conclusion that it was very much a question of the space I happened to be physically occupying . . .'

It's this *spatial* sense of being I'm working my way into up here on the Labrador plateau.

I'm remembering another book read when I was a youngster, and that may have marked me more than I've realised: Chekhov's *The Steppe*. What you've got there is exposure to an unknown territory, the freshness of images rising up directly out of the ground. No overlaid style, rather something like a physics, mind physics, word physics. None of that stale literature with its dead worlds. Something farther out, that relates you to the universe.

I've been moving out in concentric circles from my room. At first I just strolled about the town, then I went out to the mines. For the last few days I've been going out farther still.

And the plateau's opening.

And I'm opening up with it.

In *The Way of the White Clouds*, talking of the Tibetan landscape, Anagarika Govinda speaks of the transformation of consciousness brought on by the physical effects of high altitude and certain meteorological conditions.

It's the realisation of this relationship between the physical, the psychic and spiritual that is at the origin of yoga, the 'whole way' of yoga implying breathing practice, postures, mental concentration, serenity, creative imagination and spiritual awakening.

A basic practice, which only seems exotic and impossible to us because our culture destroys the very space in which it can take place: the space of solitude and silence.

In the kind of context I'm trying to describe, not only is the absence of other minds not to be regretted, it's a relief. It's this absence which allows you to get rid of the conventional tools of communication, the conceptual system necessary for ordinary social discourse, as well as a lot of secondary art. You feel your way into other dimensions. Which doesn't mean you get all wrapped up in states of consciousness. No. You move out of the domain of consciousness into a sense of immediate being.

It's only once you're outside the system that you begin to see things in a clear light.

As I said, work in progress.

Two characters keep crossing my mind up here.

One is John Meikle Gibb who, away back in eighteenth century Scotland, burned his Bible in a burst of antinomian enthusiasm, was condemned to death, but finally banished to America, where he joined the Indians and became a shaman among them.

The other is Comte Henri de Puyjalon who left his native Bordeaux country for Canada, ended up lighthouse-keeper on an island off Mingan, and wrote in his *Journal du Labrador* of the pleasures of living alone 'far from fools and especially semi-intellectuals'.

A shaman and a lighthouse-keeper.

The strange days of the Labrador Hôtel.

CALLING CARCAJOU

Went as far as the Caucasus mountains, saw the Scyths, the Massagets and the Indians.

Rabelais

I thought it was time I got social again.

I had introductions to families at the Schefferville reservation, so I went over to say hello.

The Schefferville reservation differs from the Seven Islands and the Mingan reservations in this, that among the huts and shacks you see the occasional tepee. They even say that some Indians here prefer to live in their tent and leave the shack to their dogs . .

Old Man Falconer has a tent planted next to his family's shack, and he spends most of his time in there. An old, very old leathery-faced man with a nose like a great potato on him, Old Falconer is a Naskapi. He came down to Schefferville when the Hudson's Bay closed its trading post at Fort Mackenzie. He came down, with the others, but he says he 'left his soul up there'.

I'm in Old Man Falconer's tent with two or three Indians and the old man is telling a story, he's telling a whole rigmarole of stories, about Carcajou.

Carcajou? Who's he?

Carcajou is the wolverine, but he's also the Trickster, always running around the world, always jumping about from place to place, always getting mixed up, and then getting unmixed again. Whatever happens, always making it, always merry and bright, always full of tricks.

What does Carcajou do? He de-inflates the culture. He makes you get your feet back on the ground.

Old Falconer says there aren't many wolverines around any more. All gone up North. Didn't like the priests' holy water.

But Carcajou's still around, you bet.

All you need's a little memory and a little imagination.

Old Man Falconer has plenty of both.

He tells his story.

We listen.

'Carcajou, you comin'?'

'Yep, man, I'm a-comin'.'

'Carcajou!'

'Hey, hey, I'm a-comin', I'm a-comin'. Just got all the fuzz to get through, all the malarkey, just gimme time, boy, just gimme *time*, I'll be right wid ya, I'm a comin', I'm a-comin' on the low road, where there's no code, I'm a-comin'.'

Carcajou is on the go.

Proot-proot, proot-proot, proot-proot-proot.

That's him. Farting all the time. As usual.

Proot-proot, proot-proot.

There he is. Large as life. And twice as handsome.

Proot-proot, proot-proot.

Carcajou turns round to his arse and he says:

'OK, whadowedonow?'

No answer.

Carcajou, who knows what's what, feeds his arse-hole with a little fat.

'Go and have fun in Goose Bay.'

'I already thoughda that,' says Carcajou, and he runs off so fast he knocks into a tree.

'Oops, sorry pal. Who're you?'

'Birch.'

Hearing this, Carcajou knows he's going in the right direction, so he makes off again.

Proot-proot, proot-proot.

We're still farting along the trail, hey, hey.

He sees some ducks.

The ducks start talking all at once, pointing at his belly.

'What you got there?'

'Songs, people. I got a bellyful of songs. Bring on the dancing girls and I'll sing for me supper, hey, hey.'

Always laughing, that guy.

The prettiest ducks start dancing in a circle.

'Shut your eyes,' says Carcajou. 'Shut your eyes, sweetie pies, shut your ey-es,' he croons.

All those pretty ducks shut their eyes and keep dancing.

Carcajou gobbles 'em up, one at a time, hey, hey.

Then he gets on the go again.

He sees a rock moving.

A *rock* moving?

He pretends to walk past it, then swivels round fast.

'I saw you. You moved!'

'Who moved?' says the rock.

'You talk too!' says Carcajou.

'OK, so I move and I talk, so what?'

'Crazy rock,' says Carcajou, 'you want to travel, you better come with me.'

'Suits me,' says the rock.

So Carcajou pads along, humming a little tune, and the rock rolls along beside him.

They meet a crow.

'Hello, mister, what's your name when you're at home?'

'Kujkynnjaku,' says the crow.

'What's that?'

'Kujkynnjaku.'

'Hmm. Where from?'

'Kamchatka.'

'Aha, where all the good poetry comes from. Stick around, brother, we'll have fun together.'

'OK,' says the crow.

They meet a wolf.

'How are things, partner?' says Carcajou.

'I get by,' says the wolf, 'I get by.'

'What do you do for a living?'

'I prowl around the rim of the world.'

'Well, good luck,' says Carcajou.

Carcajou knew about that wolf. He was a very old wolf. He'd been prowling around ever since the flood.

They meet a band of geese.

Wild geese.

Lovely creatures all.

Especially the little one with the green eyes.

'What's your name?' asks Carcajou.

'Bright Eyes,' says the little goose.

Carcajou invites her into the wood.

A strange creature would be born of that union.

'Call him See-the-World,' cried Carcajou, as the goose flew off into the blue.

And they all went down to the beach.

Carcajou, the crow and the wandering rock.

Carcajou pulled out a bottle of rye from his pocket.

Passed it to the crow.

The crow winked, took a gulp, and passed the bottle to the rock.

The rock said he didn't drink.

'Yeah, we know,' says Carcajou, 'you're stoned outa your mind all the time.'

He took another slug himself.

Ho hum.

They sat there looking at the waves.

That got wavier and wavier.

Till they saw an elegant gull toddling along the tide-line, now and then lifting a strand of seaweed, now and then flurrying its wings, now and then taking a fast little flight over the sea.

That got Carcajou on the go again.

'What's your name, beauty?'

'Wings of Tao.'

'Like to come along with us?'

'Where you going?'

'I don't know, but we'll get there.'

'I'll come,' said the gull, 'but let's keep to the edges. Too far inland I stifle.'

'OK with me,' says Carcajou, always willing to oblige.

Last I saw of Carcajou, the crow, the rock and the gull, they were travelling in Indian file along the shore.

The rock was just rolling along as usual.

The crow was deep in meditation.

The gull had its eyes wide open and was sniffing the breeze.

Carcajou was trotting along, singing a little song and wriggling his arse in time to the tune. As he disappeared over the horizon, he let loose one last profligate little fart.

AT INDIAN HOUSE LAKE

Somewhere, someone is speaking. In the North, the tribe of the sacred stone is speaking. You will hear someone, somewhere, speaking.

Amerindian poem — Sioux

Whenever and wherever an empty space occurs in our civilisation, instead of seeing in it a chance to deepen our sense of life, we can't wait to fill it up with noise, playthings and 'culture'.

That's why we need places like Indian House Lake.

Places where we can *listen to the world.*

Indian House Lake.

It was the Hudson's Bay man, John Maclean, who named it so in his notes, 'from the skeleton Indian tepees upon the promontories'.

When these tepees were lived in, the place was called in Montagnais *Mushua Nipi*, 'the lake of the land without trees'.

All this high plateau, still cold from the Ice Age, with its lichens, shrubs and scattered boulders, was a sanctuary: the caribou paradise, ruled over, *breathed* over by Attiknapeo, the Caribou Man.

Great herds of caribou gathered here, on their North-South, South-North migrations. And men gathered here too: Montagnais, Naskapi, Eskimo — for the hunt, and to exchange tobacco, skins, ivory.

'Countless multitudes of caribou have been slain upon Indian House Lake, so many indeed that the place has become historic,' writes Pritchard in *Through Trackless Labrador.*

'The place had become historic,' says Pritchard. What does that mean? With us, a place becomes historic when it's marked by an event or a series of events. But when Jean-Baptiste Mackenzie spoke to me about Indian House Lake, he wasn't thinking in terms of event. His sense of history was still infused with myth. In the same way, religion and economy weren't separate in his mind — at least in the depths of his mind, where his dreams still smouldered. There was a *wholeness* there. Beyond any mere sentimental evocation, beyond any anthropological study, is there any chance of such a wholeness for us? Or are we bound just to try and do the best we can with our divisions and contradictions?

Maybe we can at least learn to listen again to the world. Who knows into what secrets that may lead us.

Listening to the world . . .

I'm thinking of Black Elk's great vision:

'Now suddenly there was nothing but a world of cloud, and we were alone there in the middle of a great white plain with snowy hills and mountains staring at us, and it was very still, but *there were whispers.*'

I'm thinking of that vision, and of this poem:

Listen old man listen
listen without moving
a long time, long time listen
on the path of the rushing wind listen
where all the winds come together listen
listen old man listen
be very old and listen.

The yoga of Indian House Lake . . .

I admit that the word 'yoga' bothers me. I'd like something more ordinary.

Let's just say: sitting still, listening in, letting the wholeness take over.

All afternoon I sit there, listening.

With evening falling, I murmur this into the wind:

I'm living today
but I won't always be living
red sun, you'll remain
white moon, you'll remain
dark earth, you'll remain

THE GOOSE BAY COMPANIONS

That's where I invent a Casino, a Winter station for those who have come through.

Tristan Corbière

Just below Livingstone, at mileage 101, on the way down from Schefferville, a road leaves from the railway track. On the right day, there's a bus for Goose Bay.

That road to Goose Bay lies between the 53rd and 54th parallel, and you go from longitude 66 to longitude 60, passing through Muskrat Falls, Lake Winokapau and Lake Gull.

Travelling along it, I had an Indian poem in my head:

Out of the depths
they're on their way
old men from under the earth
they're on their way
with red circles painted on their bodies
they're on their way
at the centre of the spirit-place
they're on their way
on the red road, the good red road
they're on their way

Goose Bay that morning was a sight for sore eyes. No matter where you turned, there were fellows with long beards and haggard eyes, surrounded by camping equipment, rolls of maps and geiger counters. Prospectors and surveyors, just out of the woods. All of these were *kabloonamiut* (Eskimo for 'people with big eyebrows', that is, white men). But there were a lot of Indians and Eskimo around too, from hunters to aerodrome mechanics.

It was at a bar near the airport I met Scott Macpherson:

'You new here?'

'Yes.'

'Welcome to the NUBA.'

'Tell me what it is first.'

'Northern Ungava Bushmen Association.'

'Bushmen?'

'Bush is like when you're whacked, a bit off your rocker, been too long in the woods.'

'A lot of people up here like that?'

'Man, *everybody* up here's like that. The Eskimo and the Indians, they're born that way. We *get* that way.'

He showed me his collection of specimens. He'd been up in the Ungava prospecting for asbestos and nickel in the interests of a company down in Montreal.

'Maybe there's gold too under that there ice.'

We were joined by a man who turned out to be a bush pilot.

'Meet Jim Murphy, alias Lucky.'

I asked Murphy about flying in that territory.

'Not too easy. First there's the mist. Then the Summer storms over the lakes. There's worse than storms and mist, though. The whiteout.'

'The *whiteout*?'

'Same as blackout, only the other way round. Too much light. The snow dazzles you. You can't see.'

'What kind of plane you got?'

'A little Cesna. Single motor. It'll go anywhere, sea or land. I can fix floats on her, skis on her, anything. Take you anywhere. You want to go somewhere?'

'Maybe later, along the coast.'

'No problem. Season's over for me. I'm available.'

Murphy said to come over to his place that night, have a drink and talk. Okay.

N.A.N.R.

Northern Affairs and National Resources.

D.N.A.

Department of Northern Affairs.

T.N.L.

Terre-Neuve et Labrador.

The Northern land is being taken in hand.

But essentially, Goose Bay is still a passing-through place. The wild goose still passes through here on its way to Walden Pond and beyond.

To counteract those other bureaus, maybe we should set up a *Bureau de la Science du Passage* or a *Centre for Geopoetic Research . . .*

As I wander round the place, I imagine a company of human 'wild geese' gathered from all over the world, forming an archipelago of live minds. Not so much artists as explorers of being and nothingness. Erratics and extravagants, looking for new configurations, outwith the field of ordinary culture.

New mental energies. Fresh air blowing over the world!

OK, wishful thinking.

I know it's going to be end city for a long time yet.

I went to Murphy's place that night.

He had a wonderful radio that could pick up all the stations in Quebec and Labrador.

He could get the Eskimo stations at Ivujivik, Koartak, Akulivik, Aupaluk, Leaf Bay, Payne Bay, George River, Poste-de-la-Baleine, Inukjuak, Povunghituk, Sugluk, Wakeham Bay and Fort Chimo.

He could get the Indian stations at Caughnawaga, Natashquan, Mingan, La Romaine and Saint-Augustin.

He could get the French stations at Montreal, Maniwaki, Havre-Saint-Pierre, Iles-de-la-Madeleine, Gagnon, Fort Coulonge, Fermont, Rimouski, Schefferville, Senneterre and Châteauguay.

With Murphy's radio, you could also send messages out. Using the international code, I sent out this:

Charlie uniform lima tango uniform romeo echo stop.

Alpha November alpha romeo Charlie hôtel India sierra tango echo stop.

Papa lima alpha November echo tango alpha India romeo echo over.

Will the message be received?

Maybe not.

But we'll keep trying.

ARCTIC CHRONICLES

The word sila *has three meanings: world, time, intelligence.*

Kuud Rasmussen

First there was the ice, then came the Eskimo.

Where the Eskimo came from, God only knows — the secret's buried somewhere beyond Beringia — but they ended up *Labradoremuit*, Labrador people.

In Winter, they hunted furs; in Spring they went seal-hunting, and they fished for sea-trout and cod; in Summer they caught sea-birds and gathered blueberries in the tundra. They lived in ice-houses (*iglovigak*) or in turf-houses (*iglosoak*) and in skin-tents.

The first Europeans on the scene were Vikings, out from Greenland:

Nu er at segja af Karlsefni at hann for sudr fyrir landit ok Snorri ok Bjarni med sinu folki peir foru lengi ok allt par til . . .

(Now it must be told that Karlsefni travelled South, along with Snorri, Bjarni and all his people. They sailed a long time, till . . .)

They had a Scotsman with them, picked up somewhere in the Hebrides, who wandered off into the woods as soon as he got ashore and managed to find the wherewithall to get maundering drunk.

The Norseman had a few skirmishes with the Eskimo, but those skimps of men (*skraeling*, said the Vikings) turned out to be as ferocious as hell, so they decided to leave them alone and went back to their farms.

After that, there were wild Basques from Bayonne, Biarritz and St Jean-de-Luz, whalers, followed in the same vocation by long-haired, grey-eyed Bretons from Paimpol and the Ile Bréhat. For a long time after they'd gone, there were still piles of whalebone marking where they'd built their stations, at Forteau, Red Bay, Brador.

At the end of the seventeenth century, Augustin Legardeur, *Sieur de Courtemanche*, obtained the privilege of fishing and engaging in commerce in the Straits of Belle-Ile. He and his son-in-law Martel de Brouage built a fort in the Baie Phélypeaux that became a trade centre for the South Labrador people. They sent whalebone and seal-oil to France. By 1706 there was a concession at Saint Paul 'in the land of the Eskimos', between Mingan and Belle-Ile. Other concessions went as far as Central Labrador, to the Baie des Esquimaux.

The year 1763 saw the end of French influence, and a horde of adventurers from England, Scotland, Ireland and the American colonies took over. Sir Hugh Palliser, governor of Newfoundland, deplored 'the mixed multitudes now resorting to the new Northern banks about the Straits of Belle-Ile, composed of the very scum from the different colonies'.

At the head of a band of Scots-Irish and Indians, a certain Cartwright had a line of trading posts stretching from St Charles to Sandwich Bay. A rogue and a rascal, this Cartwright, out for every penny he could get, but his journal shows that he also had an eye to other things. The wild coast didn't leave him indifferent:

'On August 10th,' he writes, 'we saw a flock of curlews that may have been a mile long and nearly as broad. There must have been four or five thousand of them. The sum total of their notes sounded like the wind whistling through the ropes of a thousand-ton vessel.'

By the end of the eighteenth century, the whole coast South of Battle Harbour was overrun by Europeans and Americans. They were divided into *liveyres*, stationers and floaters. The *liveyres* (Franco-English, from 'live here') hunted seals and fur-bearing animals, and fished for cod and salmon; they also had little gardens made of soil scraped together here and there. The stationers, mainly from Newfoundland and the North bank of the St Lawrence, stayed for the fishing season. As to the floaters, they had no settlements at all, they came up in Canadian *goëlettes* and fished from doris for greenfish (*morue verte*).

Stationers and floaters gradually moved up farther and farther North — up to Nashvak, Ryan's Bay and Komaktorvik. They came in increasing numbers, and in bigger and bigger boats.

The Hudson's Bay Company built its first post at Rigolet in 1832, and they soon spread out to Nashvak and Ramah.

All those people on the coast . . .

But there was plenty of space between them, and Labrador was still an isolated place. Before 1901, mail came once a year. If you went 'up the coast', you had to be able to rough it, on your own.

It was too tough, even for the Eskimo. They were no longer what they had been — typhoid, drink, diphtheria, influenza and missionary education had seen to that. Instead of living scattered all over the landscape, they now huddled permanently in communities. The Northern fiords, those that wound into the Torngat Mountains, were deserted. In 1919, an influenza epidemic wiped out Okkak. A lone dog stayed at Hebron. Everybody had gone South. To Happy Valley, for example, near Goose Bay. Good wages, good houses, entertainment:

I'm H-A-P-P-Y
I'm H-A-P-P-Y
I know I am I'm sure I am
I'm H-A-P-P-Y

Imagine that sung by Harry the Eskimo to the jolly sounds of an evangelical squeeze-box.

The Hudson's Bay post at Nashvak closed down in 1906. The year 1908 saw the closing of the post at Ramah.

Nowadays the whole territory North of Nain 'lies lone and frigid in its polar wastes' (I'm quoting Wallace, *The Long Labrador Trail*).

So we've come full circle.

Back at the beginning.

THE NAKED EARTH

Earth, sea, fire, wind — singing into the white act.

Dylan Thomas

I began taking trips with Lucky up the coast:

Aulatsik Island
The Kiglapaits
The Okkak Islands
Cod Island
The Kaumajets
Hebron Fiord
Saglek Bay
Ramah Bay
Nashvak Bay
The Torngats
Cape White
Ryan's Bay
Killinek . . .

It is all very beautiful and totally desolate.

'The Labrador coast,' writes a geologist, 'is still one of the most bold and rugged in the whole world. The bareness of the rocks, their freedom from obscuring forest and turf, helps the long coast to tell its own geological story. Mother Nature has here taken off more than the usual amount of clothing which she is wont to bestow on the land elsewhere, and the autographed story of the ages is imprinted on her naked bones.'

How to get into that nakedness, into that emptiness?
Live with it and say it?
Flying up the coast, over the ice-blue sea of Labrador, I had

Eskimo shaman poems in my head:

The great sea
has sent me adrift
it moves me
as the weed in a great river
earth and the great weather
move me
they have carried me away
they move my inward parts with joy

Spaced-out poems, way beyond the person. To stand up to a landscape such as this, it takes a poetry close to the bone and open to the winds.

I was looking for a place to set myself down in. For a night and a day. In darkness and in light.

Nashvak seemed a good choice.

I spent a night, a long night, walking in the arctic stillness.

In that sanctuary of birds.

Trying to get on to the farthest wave-length:

Here on the Labrador
in the twilight watching countless birds
settled and asleep
only a few still on the wing
that passing flight of Sabine gulls

is this a death?
or the prelude to another life?

the question is all too heavy
breenges

into the rippling silence
like a bull into china
better simply to wait
taking pleasure in the twilight

tongues of water
tongues of water from the sea of ice
running up the bays and fiords
lapping against the archaean rocks
will say the poem beyond the questioning

the birds are asleep
geese, duck, brant, teal, plover
all are asleep
as though this land were one great sanctuary

a place to rest
on the long trail of the migrations

a place to rest
yet I am restless

here in the stillness
half-way between the Old World and the New
moving in deeper
ever deeper
into a world
that is neither old nor new

a world
neither old nor new
on the bird path
feeling it out

. . .

dawn comes
with the cry of the wild goose

UNGAVA

Blue, as of a secret place.
Wallace Stevens

The wind kept blowing: *megamoowessoo, megamoowessoo* . . . Up here on the bay of Ungava at this time of the year, there's a gale blowing six days out of seven.

Ungava means, in Eskimo, 'the farthest place'.

But civilisation has reached even the 'farthest place', in the form of an agglomeration known as Fort Chimo.

Fort Chimo, on the banks of the River Koksoak, is a huddle of red and green shacks, with hangars interspersed, and a handful of more permanent houses on the edge. There are even some dwellings shaped like igloos, so the old Eskimos will feel at home.

It's civilised, all right. You can play billiards, you can play Bingo. You can go to the cinema run by the Catholic Mission. You can get Welfare. You won't see any Eskimo going at it white-fanged at whale or caribou meat. Na, na. They eat kraft, baloney and hot-dogs plastered with HP sauce like everybody else. Which leads to further progress: every year there's a Dental Health Week ('Smile, baby, smile!').

I sit here in a hut lent me by an anthropologist of the university of Laval, listening to the snowy wind.

On the table in front of me, there's a copy of Humboldt's *Cosmos* and a piece of labradorite.

Labradorite?

When the molten earth finally froze, it turned into mineral masses such as quartz, feldspath, mica and hornblende.

Labradorite is a variety of feldspath.

When white light penetrates into its glassy surface, it's broken up into *a multiplicity of blue flashes.*

I pick up that piece of labradorite every now and then, and let the light play through it.

Last night I had a dream.

I was with an Eskimo.

We were at a table, drinking and talking.

He said his drunkenness had now reached its ultimate stage.

'It's the *skinadur,'* he said.

The transcendental phase.

If he was on the harpooning board now, a voice would say to him: 'Don't kill the whale. Here's your chance to reach Tamanika.'

'Where's Tamanika?' I asked.

'Tamanika's nowhere,' he said.

I've been dreaming a good deal recently. Dream after dream. As if something was trying to get through from way back in my mind. Or from somewhere else.

Here's a dream from a couple of nights back.

I'd been invited by this Centre for Spiritual Studies in England.

I find myself in a town. I take a taxi. We come to the house where the conference is to be held. It's situated on a river bank, on a promontory. I'm disappointed. I'd thought it was on the edge of the ocean. It looks drab too. But there are mountains, snow-capped, on the horizon.

I'm sitting in the lounge, waiting for the conference to begin. People are playing cards, pukka type English people, with silver-plated heirlooms as stakes. Two men are seated close beside me. On the one hand, an old bore of a gentleman, esoteric occultist of some kind; on the other, a pleasant, superficial fellow, positivistic-scientific sort.

Absolutely nothing doing.

Later on, I'm in my room. It has storm windows, with three layers of thick glass.

A girl comes in. She undresses. She has *blue breasts.*

The mad son of the lady-organiser is wandering about the house. He stops outside my door, making excited signs that something unusual and anti-social is going on inside my room.

The next scene I see from a distance. There's me, the girl, and a hubbub of people.

I'm indifferent to everything except the blue breasts.

Blue things flash across my path every now and then, either in dream or in the waking state.

It began in Glasgow. The blue sari on the bridge . . .

Then there was the dream in which I saw a stone, and the stone broke, and inside there was that strange blue light.

And there was that morning in the Botanic Gardens when I came across the blue flowers of the Tibetan poppy.

These appearances usually occur at times of distress.

As recently, when I was standing one morning at the window of a house in Brittany, and a blue jay alighted just in front of it.

These blue signs put me back on the *deep path*.

The most detailed account of the 'deep path' is probably the *Tibetan Book of the Dead*, which tells of the forty-nine days' journey of the soul to its home. This soul-journey is called the *bardo*, and the stages along the way are accompanied by different experiences of light and colour.

No need to interpret the *bardo* purely in terms of after death. It's just that 'life' consists mainly of secondary pursuits and secondary discourse, it's only when you're 'dead', dead to that pseudo-living, that you are able, at last, to get into some more fundamental experience, have some inkling of the 'radiant path of knowledge'.

The wind's blowing over the Ungava, and it's a long evening at Fort Chimo, somewhere in the big world-night.

Just a few yards away — I get snatches of it — an Eskimo rock band is thumping out *Polar Blues.*

I sit at the window all night.

The sounds of the rockapocalypse die out about one o'clock.

I sit listening to the wind.

Turning the piece of labradorite in my hand.

At dawn, I hear a gull cry, and I think of Max Stirner's *The Self and its Own*: 'The meaning of a cry of joy beyond all thought, the immense meaning which couldn't be known while men were still going through the long night of thought and faith.'

Can we get out of that 'long night' now?

Maybe — if we've done enough work in a field that is neither that of thought nor of faith.

The great work-field.

A kind of Labrador.

I go out to salute the morning and the world.

And the wind brings me a poem, like a great waking dream, in which 'the man looking for the North' takes on the shape of one of those Norse travellers such as Erik the Red or Karl Karlsefni who reached Labrador about the year 1000.

In the space won at the end of the personal journey, identities and times are mingled.

Beyond ourselves, then, let's listen to the poem.

LABRADOR
OR
THE WAKING DREAM

1

Another dawn
out from Greenland
whales bellowing in the icy sea
and the vast sky
resounding with wind

once more I felt that breadth of mind
like being drunk
but this was colder and more clear
than anything
that might come out of a jug
it was what I'd always lived for
what I always will *live for*
till they throw me
into the trough of the waves
I was used to dance over

there are some who delight
in the storm of swords
and those who make
public speech with words
these are the warriors and the governors
I have preferred other ways
the lonely ways of the sky of sands
the gull path

in all my lonely ongoings
I have thought of many things
I have thought of the earth
in its beginnings

when time was a sequence of cold dawns
and space was full of
the wings of hallucinated birds
I have dreamed of a primal place
a place of rocks, quick streams and emptiness
each morning
the sun rising in the chill sea of the East
and throughout the long day throbbing
above the rocks, above the waters

the earth then was a nameless place
I have been in love with nameless places
now there are too many names
Norway of the blue streams
is rank with names
the Hebrides and even Greenland
names, names, names
and a welter of angry clamorings
it was time to move farther West

and so another dawn
out from Greenland
and still no other land in sight
only the green waves and the wind
and a vision in the mind.

2

I also named a place
a place of great rocks
and the sun glinting on them

a place filled
with a rush and a flowing of waters
I called it The Marvellous Shore

I lived a Winter there
it was a time of white silence
I carved a poem on the rocks
in praise of Winter and the white silence
the best runes I ever cut

men with long eyes and high cheek-bones
came to visit me
I gave them cloth
they gave me skins
there was peace between us

when Spring came
all the streams running with light
and the big river reflecting the sky
I travelled farther South
into a land of forest
I met red men there
dressed like birds

I was aware of a new land
a new world
but I was loathe to name it too soon
simply content to use my senses
feeling my way
step by step into the reality

I was no longer Christian
nor yet had I gone back to Thor
there was something else
calling to me
calling me out
and waiting, perhaps, to be called

something sensual
and yet abstract
something fearsome and yet beautiful
it was beyond me
and yet
more myself than myself

I thought of talks in Norway
the talk of poets and of thinkers
I thought of high talk in the Hebrides

here was no place for Christ or Thor
here the earth worked out its destiny
its destiny of rocks and trees
and sunlight and darkness
worked out its destiny in silence
I tried to learn
the language of that silence
more difficult than the Latin
I learned in Bergen
or the Irish in Dublin.

3

A whole new field
in which to labour and to think
and with every step I took
I knew a singular health
mind every day more sharp, more clear

I hazarded some more names
(after weighing them carefully each one
trying them out in my mind
and on my tongue):

Great Whale River, Eskimo Point
Indian House Lake, Caribou Pass
but still no name for the whole
I was willing to name the parts
but not the whole

a man needs to fix his knowledge
but he also needs an emptiness
in which to move

I lived and moved
as I had never done before
became a little more than human even
knew a larger identity

the tracks of caribou in the snow
the flying of wild geese

the red Autumn of the maple tree
bitten by frost
all these became more real to me
more really me
than my very name

I found myself saying things like
'at one with the spirit of the land'
but there was no 'spirit', none
that was outworn language
and this was a new world
and my mind was, almost, a new mind
there was no such thing as 'spirit'
only the blue tracks in the snow
the flying of the geese
the frost-bitten leaf

religion and philosophy
what I'd learned in the churches and the schools
were all too heavy
for this travelling life
all that remained to me was poetry
but a poetry
as unobtrusive as breathing
a poetry like the wind
and the maple leaf
that I spoke to myself
moving over the land

I am an old man now
an old man very old
I have scratched these runes on a rock

to be my testament
perhaps no one will read them
and that is no matter
let them stand on the rock
beside the scratchings of the ice
open to wind and weather.